ALSO BY MATTHEW VOLLMER

FICTION & NON-FICTION

Future Missionaries of America

inscriptions for headstones

Gateway to Paradise

Permanent Exhibit

ANTHOLOGIES

Fakes: An Anthology of Pseudo Interviews, Faux-Lectures, Quasi-Letters, "Found" Texts, and Other Fraudulent Artifacts
(Co-edited with David Shields)

A Book of Uncommon Prayer

THIS WORLD IS NOT YOUR HOME

THIS WORLD IS NOT YOUR HOME

Essays, Stories, and Reports

MATTHEW VOLLMER

The following sections of this book have been previously published
in different form: "Supermoon" in *StoryQuarterly*; "This World Is Not
Your Home" in *Ploughshares*; "How to Write a Love Story" in *Epoch*;
"Notes for an Essay on Special Music" at *Essay Daily*; "Keeper of the
Flame" in *New England Review* and *Best American Essays 2013*; "NeVer
ForgeT" in *Ecotone*; "The Other, Invented Man" in *The Sun*; "Ghost
House" (as "101 Oak Street") in *Territory*; "Music of the Spheres: A
Meditation on NASA's Symphonies of the Planets" and "Over the
River and Through the Woods" in *The Normal School*.

Published in the United States by EastOver Press.

eastoverpress.com

ISBN 978-1-934894-72-9

Book design by Evan Lavender-Smith and Jackson Smith.

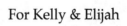

For Kelly & Elijah

CONTENTS

THIS WORLD IS NOT YOUR HOME

SUPERMOON

They had just finished eating—the man and woman and their son—at their favorite Mexican restaurant, where, even though they hadn't quite cleaned their plates, they complained that they'd eaten too much, which was a signal for the man to say, as he always did, "Time to visit the vomitorium." Though the man knew that feasting was an important part of high culture in ancient Rome and that the wealthy enjoyed slathering wild boar and venison with fermented fish intestines, he also knew, because he'd consulted his phone during a previous visit to this same restaurant, that feasters did not excuse themselves, waving away slaves who'd been enlisted to brush crumbs and bits of bones from their faces, in order to visit a system of tureens reserved especially for regurgitating food, thereby allowing vomiters to return with vigor to their indulgences. The man knew that the word *vomitorium* actually described the entryways of ancient Roman amphitheaters. But because *vomitorium* was a word that made both his wife and son shake their heads and laugh despite themselves, he said it, and the trio took it as their cue to leave.

On the way home the woman suggested that they should all go for a walk; after all, the dog had been left inside all day and could use some fresh air, and as good as it might sound to lie down, the family might better aid their digestion by perambulating the neighborhood. This sounded like a good idea to the man, but once he parked the car in the driveway, the boy slung open the door and scampered toward the house, and by the time his parents made it inside he had already resumed the playing of whatever video game he'd most recently downloaded to his tablet computer, the one that required him to tap and swipe the screen of the device with the relentless tenacity of a madman. The woman shrugged. The man hooked the dog's collar to a leash. And because they had recently agreed that twelve was an appropriate age to leave the boy alone in a house for short periods of time, they told him they'd be back in a little while and left without him.

*

At first, the man and woman walked without talking, and this, the man thought, was fine. Nice, even. The man had always enjoyed taking walks with the woman, and she with him. Though the two were different in many ways, and though she was half an inch taller and her legs were longer, the couple walked at the same brisk pace—the woman often noted that they shared a similar stride—and so walking together, though they never held hands, as this had the tendency to introduce an awkwardness that impeded their gait, felt completely natural.

At the crest of the hill, the woman sighed heavily, and when the man asked what was wrong, she said she was in a funk.

Instead of asking her to talk more about this funk, the man said something like, "Me, too" or, in a way that suggested he was in the same boat, "Tell me about it." It would be easy to imagine that the man had good intentions for claiming a funk of his own, and that by commiserating with his wife, he might have been curating a little funk-sharing space, one they might inhabit together and thereby lift one another's spirits, but the truth was, the man had gotten temporarily caught up—as he sometimes did—in a kind of playful but ultimately self-serving brand of spousal antagonism. After all, it was beyond ludicrous to think that even if he did have a funk to call his own that it could compare to hers, which was a funk that happened to be six months in the making, a funk that, were it a human baby, would soon have the strength and wherewithal to crawl around on its own. This funk had been born, more or less, at the end of the previous winter, when the man and woman went to a local breast imaging center and sat in a waiting room where a bald, goateed man in overalls and a satin Harley Davidson jacket held a little girl on his knee while the old woman next to him—head wrapped in a scarf, eyebrowless face forcibly placid—drank Styrofoam cup after Styrofoam cup of medicine.

At that point, the woman squeezed the man's hand. He squeezed back and said, "It's going to be okay," and then a nurse called the woman's name and she left the room. Two days later, the woman received a call from the radiologist, who said everything was fine, that there were some calcifications in both breasts, nothing major, but something to keep an eye on, which was something of a relief, at least for the next forty-eight hours, until the woman got another call, and the same doctor said that he'd been having some second thoughts, and that he'd given the mammogram to another radiologist, one who had a bit more experience, and this radiologist had said something like, "Well, fifty percent of doctors who know what they're looking at would tell you that it looks like you might wanna biopsy, and the other fifty percent would be content to watch and wait," and "If it were me, I'd biopsy," and so a week or so later the doctors removed tissue from one of the breasts and sent it to a lab, where it tested positive for a certain kind of noninvasive breast cancer, specifically a kind that begins in the milk ducts.

Before the woman had learned of this new development, she had decided—because it was the most conservative and therefore safest approach—that if the news were bad, she would elect to undergo a double mastectomy with reconstruction, a process that subsequently involved visits to a number of doctors, including a family physician, an oncologist, a breast surgeon, a plastic surgeon, a radiation oncologist, and a regular oncologist, who after learning that the wife had suffered four miscarriages, surmised that the flood of estrogen of a full-blown pregnancy might have been just the thing to cause the cells in those milk ducts to spread. Other doctors wrote on white boards, drawing normal-looking cells and cells that had mutated. They suggested books for the woman to read. They asked the same questions that nurses had just asked. They made inquiries about family history and medications. During exactly zero of these visits had the woman explained that she'd been writing a book about the rhetoric of breast cancer survivors, a project whose origins could likely be traced back to the fact that the woman's mother had died when she was only forty-six years of age, and that the woman had been fourteen at the time, and that this event had shaped her life to a profound degree, since for years afterward she privately grieved for her mother, filling journals with writing, notebooks upon notebooks she still kept but never read and never showed anyone. It goes without saying, then, that the woman's diagnosis had been devastating— she had lain for a long time in the middle of the day on the bed with the man, crying and dabbing her eyes and saying things like, "Maybe there's a silver lining to all this," because they'd discovered it before it had become invasive, and then thinking of a world in which her son didn't have a mom, and crying some more, and the man remembered a story his wife had told him long ago about sitting alone on the floor of her living room not long after her mother had died, watching cartoons with tears streaming down her face, while eating an ice cream pie that had been delivered by her father's new girlfriend. So, yes, the news had been devastating. The procedure itself had also been painful— the first surgery involved not only the removal of breast tissue but the insertion of expanders to stretch her pectoral muscles—and exhausting—the woman had to sleep in a recliner for four weeks—and messy—tubes draining blood and liquid from wounds into little squeeze bottles that had to be emptied twice a day—and boring—it turned out a person could only watch so much TV before you felt like you were going insane—and frustrating—she longed to exercise but couldn't run for a month, and then, once she'd returned to her previous form, the second surgery, during which the expanders would be replaced with gel packs, she'd had to give up running again. This, more or less, was the extent of the woman's funk, which, it is perhaps plain to see, the man was foolish to have equated with his own, even—and perhaps especially if—he was joking.

The couple continued to walk in silence. This silence, though, wasn't like before. It wasn't comfortable. At least not for the man. Did the woman now resent his presence? Did she wish she'd stayed at the house—or that he hadn't come along? He couldn't be sure. The only thing he could say with absolute certainty was that the evening through which they were walking was, without question, incredibly beautiful. In the distance, unseen children were laughing and screaming happily—the man imagined a game of chase or hide-and-go-seek while the children's parents sipped cocktails or stood over flaming grills. Fireflies pulsed in the air: little intermittent flashes of green. One might even say—as the man couldn't help but think—that they were walking right through the middle of a quintessential summer evening, as if the night itself was pulling out all the stops to put on the performance of the season. The man and woman turned a corner. A soft breeze rustled the leaves of a tree, which diffused a yellow glow. Past the tree, they could see in the sky a low, full moon: a bright and impossibly huge sphere hovering above the neighborhood, illuminating the algae-blanketed pond across the street, riming the dark-green fields beyond. The man pointed skyward. The woman said, "Wow." The fact that they had both been rendered speechless gave the man hope; maybe, he thought, the beauty they'd encountered during this little stroll would erase the memory of his ineptitude. He kept quiet, so as not to infringe on an unspoken truce. He thought about taking a picture and instinctively patted his pockets to locate his phone, which he remembered having left in the bedroom to charge. And that was okay. It wasn't possible to take a good picture of the moon, anyway—at least not with his phone.

As the couple approached their house, a light in the living room snapped on, followed shortly by another light downstairs. Initially, the man figured the appearance of a sequence of lights in their house could be easily explained: his son likely wandering through rooms, looking for a cord so he could charge the dying battery of the tablet computer. Then again, the man thought, it could've been anybody. For years, they'd left the front door unlocked: they would leave the house for a few minutes or a few hours or an entire day, and though they would certainly shut it, they rarely locked their front door, placing full trust in their neighbors and anyone who might wander into their cul-de-sac (proselytizers and lawn care specialists and meter readers and pizzeria employees placing hangtags on doorknobs) that they would have the good sense not to enter a home that wasn't theirs.

They heard the screams as they approached the front door. It was the boy, screaming—in a way that seemed desperate—their names, as if through force of sheer will and volume the man and woman might materialize. The man figured that the boy had somehow injured himself and remembered once when he was a kid at a church camp and how he'd ducked out of playing baseball, because he hated baseball, and returned to his room, where he'd cut himself playing with a pocket knife and started screaming bloody murder for help, and how a neighbor had appeared and said, after inspecting the injury, which turned out to be rather slight, "I thought somebody had cut their leg off." The boy, however, was not injured. He was, as he attempted to explain between exhausted sobs, *scared*; he hadn't known where his parents were. He'd tried to call his mother's phone and she hadn't answered, and he'd tried to call the father's phone, and he hadn't answered either, and because both of them had never not answered their phones, the boy had become afraid and began to entertain worst-case scenarios. It was here that the man was overcome with empathy for his son; he could remember having this exact feeling as a kid, and how terrible it had been to not know where your parents were and then imagining that something horrible had happened to them, and the more time passed without them showing up, the more real the imagined scenario became, until it had solidified itself in reality and become the only viable explanation: this was it, they were never coming back: they were gone forever. But the man and woman had returned. They were not gone forever. And so the woman hugged the boy and then the man hugged him too and then the man said I want to show you something. He took the boy's hand and led him outside, knowing that the boy was probably wondering what in the world he was doing, taking him out into the yard at this hour, at night, and then in the space between the houses across the street the man pointed, and the boy looked into the sky and saw the big bright moon.

For the most part, the couple had kept their son in the dark about the particulars of his mother's surgery. He didn't know that the entirety of his mother's breast tissue had been removed. He didn't know that a surgeon had placed expanders under her pectoral muscles and that she'd had to visit the surgeon every two weeks to receive injections that would gradually enlarge them. He'd never seen the drains where red fluid sloshed. He didn't know that the expanders had been replaced with gel packs. He didn't know that his mother would be returning to the operating room in December to remove her fallopian tubes, because that was, doctors had discovered, where ovarian cancer likely started. The boy had only known that doctors had found something in her breasts that could turn into cancer if they didn't remove it. He didn't ask any follow-ups. He was more concerned about the recliner the woman had to sleep in. Once she was done with it, she'd promised it would be his.

The man didn't explain that the moon wasn't really bigger, that its apparent enormity was merely an optical illusion. Instead, he let his son bask in the brightness, hoping that the sight of it would act like a commemorative stamp on his memory, and that someday the man would say, "Hey, remember that time when you thought we were gone and I showed you the moon?" and the boy would say, "Yeah," and then the man would tell him about how he and the boy's mother had walked together, each of them carrying silent burdens the boy had known nothing about, and the boy would remember the time when his father, who could not always be depended on to do or say the right thing, had shepherded him into the yard and pointed to the huge round rock in the sky that was reflecting the light of

the nearest star, and how the boy had wiped away his tears
to see it.

THIS WORLD IS NOT YOUR HOME

The town where you grew up—the place you'll always think of as home—has three stoplights, a grocery store, a twin cinema, a post office, two dozen churches, three banks, a hospital, a video store, a handful of gas stations, and three factories that produce custom wood furniture, Lee jeans, and outboard motors. There's a Main Street where teenagers drive Mustangs and Chevys on Friday nights, a parking lot where they raise hoods and rev engines. There's a video store with a Spy Hunter arcade game and rows of VHS boxes featuring bare-chested, bazooka-wielding hunks, flanked by brunettes in wet T-shirts. There's a Happy Flounder whose cash register is flanked by a box of Fruit Stripe gum and a canister of Lions Club Mints. There's a rec center with a public pool and basketball courts whose goals are netted with chains. There's a barbershop where old men tell stories about bear, coons, huckleberries, railroads, gardens, and the dearth or surfeit of rain. There are hot, gleaming tracks where oncoming engines flatten pennies to glossy oblongs. There are mountains—blue ridges rising above the town like the walls of a distant citadel. There are woods where you find jack-in-the-pulpit and lady's slippers and puffballs that, when squeezed, ejaculate greenish smoke. There are snakes and wasps and hog wallers, secret waterfalls and caves where outlaws once hid. There are fields whose dirt, when plowed, surrenders pottery shards, musket balls, and arrowheads: the artifacts of a Cherokee civilization whose members three centuries ago—before Andrew Jackson signed the Indian Removal Act of 1830, and before said Indians were rounded up and marched, at bayonet point, from cool, hemlock-shaded hollows to blistering Oklahoman prairies—would've outnumbered the white people living here now.

You're one of those people, and you've lived here your whole life. Even so, when you're biking down Main Street—on your sky-blue Schwinn Predator, the one with the pegs and the silver rotator cuff that allows the handlebars to spin—you feel conspicuous. Maybe it's because you don't really live *in* town but on its outskirts, in a cove at the base of a mountain. Maybe it's because you know so few town folk, while your dad—a dentist—can't go anywhere without someone stopping him, to give him a hard time about hardly working, and thus embarking upon the kind of banter in which two people engage one another in mutual but affable disparagement. Maybe it's because your family belongs to a church whose members gather together to worship on the seventh day of the week instead of the first—a church that views itself as separate from the rest of the world. Maybe it's because your best friends are a pair of sisters—a freckled blonde named Jolene, a brunette named Raylene—who live in a house on Happy Top with a trampoline and rabbit cages and a plastic clown head in the yard, which when hooked up to a hose shoots water out of its skull. Maybe it's because you don't go to your hometown's public elementary school; instead, you meet five other kids in the parking lot of the Valley Plaza every morning to carpool to another town, to a private church school in a three-room, A-frame house. There, thirty kids in grades one through eight gather to learn about the walls of Jericho, the scepter of Herod, the Ark of the Covenant, the faith of the Centurion, and the Spirit of Prophecy, which was made manifest more than a hundred years ago within a young woman named Ellen Gould White, who also happened to be one of the founders of your church, a girl who when she was nine years old was struck in the head with a rock, took ill, and never fully recovered, though at seventeen she shouted "Glory! Glory!" and was granted the first of many visions: people walked on a narrow pathway of light toward heaven; those who kept their eyes upon the illuminated body of Christ could walk without stumbling, while those who looked at their feet fell into the dark.

*

The year is 1985. You stand four feet, ten inches tall. Your father thinks you should part your hair; you prefer out of habit to comb your bangs over your eyebrows. You have a dent in your chest—the scientific term is *pectus excavatum*—that makes you self-conscious; when swimming you insist on wearing a shirt. You have a scar on your leg where, while showing off some karate moves to a friend, you simultaneously kicked and lunged, plunging the tip of a Swiss Army knife straight through your jeans, and opening up a mouth of fatty tissue in your thigh—a perforation that your father sewed shut using thread he uses to stitch holes in the mouths of his patients. You wear a shirt your mother stitched together out of fabric imprinted with tuxedoed penguins or a gray hooded sweatshirt with a black mesh crop top emblazoned with the words *Dallas* and *Cowboys.* You think of yourself as fast and elusive, and though you can't play football on a team for real because your family observes the Sabbath from Friday sundown to Saturday sundown, you dream of being so good that you'll bypass high school and college and sign a contract with the Cowboys as a walk-on, and that your athleticism will be so valued by your coaches they won't require you to attend Saturday practices.

On May 25, 1985, you'll be eleven years old.

*

You may live in the boonies—at the end of a dirt road at the bottom of a mountain, in a house on a mossy, molehill-ridden hump above two streams—but thanks to TV and *Sports Illustrated* and *Time* magazine and *People* and Walmart and Casey Kasem's *Top 40,* you're into the usual stuff. *MAD* magazine. The NFL. Michael Jackson. Rich Little. Sticks shaped like guns. Fighter jets. Ninjas. You tie T-shirts around your head, knotting the sleeves so that the head-hole stretches tight across your eyes. You fashion a pair of homemade nunchucks by sawing a broom handle in half and nailing a strip of chain to the ends. You check out a how-to book on ninjutsu from the Nantahala Regional Library that illustrates stealth tactics, including grabbing on to a gutter spout while walking up the side of a house. You check this book out again. You renew it. You dream of actual Chinese throwing stars. Of blowguns. Of swashbuckling rooftop fights during which you employ dual samurai swords to disarm your enemies.

Your younger sister likes to dress up in your mom's old heels and your dead Great-Aunt Maddie's mothbally dresses. Your mother bakes her own bread, makes clothes using a sewing machine, cross-stitches pictures of African American men eating watermelon, plays the piano for church, and runs a fundraising program for your school that involves selling boxes of oranges and grapefruit ("the citrus program," she calls it) to locals. Meanwhile, your father—a balding man with glasses, who strikes you as simultaneously nerdy and robust—spends his days staring into mouths: flesh-scapes of rotting bone, where incomprehensibly strong tongues, coated with mucous-thick yellow plaque, lap involuntarily against his rubber-gloved fingers, like quick blind slugs.

*

You enter your father's office with a sense of propriety: it's a place you might inherit, assuming you too become a dentist (which seems as likely an occupation as any), a place you can come and go and do as you please. You press the square, colored buttons on the X-ray machine, commandeer a vacant dental chair and make it rise and fall by depressing a pedal, squirt the walls or the inside of your mouth with the water hose, create a mobile indentation in the flesh of your hand by spraying it with the air gun, ride the wheeled chairs of the receptionists' area, and rummage through the treasure box, keeping the best erasers and stickers for yourself. You play with a hinged set of oversized fake teeth (ostensibly used by hygienists to model good brushing, though you've never witnessed them do this), take inventory of the refrigerator in the lab where your dad torches clay models of his patients' teeth and where his assistants often eat lunch or stir squishy green bowls of acidic-smelling impression mixture, pour yourself a Dixie cup of Diet Coke, or, best of all, flip through the channels on the little TV, which has cable. You don't have cable at home—the lines don't come out that far, plus your mother thinks you watch enough junk as it is—and so visiting the office inevitably involves watching TV, usually TBS, which means episodes of *I Dream of Jeannie* and *Bewitched*, both of which, with their benevolent sorceresses, might've been argued by your elementary school teacher to glorify and therefore make safe the idea of witchcraft. You don't worry about that, though. You like the idea of magic being real. You'd like to have your own genie. You wouldn't waste a single wish.

Your family calls your father's employees "the girls." You like the girls. The girls are locals who obtained degrees at Western Carolina or Tri-County. The girls watch soap operas and visit tanning beds and drink diet soda. They play practical jokes on each other—leaving rubber snakes in file cabinet drawers, shooting fellow staff members with water guns on their birthdays. They bring leftover cake and leave it in the lab, and Lord, yes, get yourself a piece. On Halloween, the girls dress up like tubes of toothpaste or Pippi Longstocking. Every year they present you with a birthday cake on a foiled mat from the local grocery store: Superman, Spiderman, Bugs Bunny, Snoopy. One of the girls—a white-haired woman whose husband recently retired from the railroad and now watches Cincinnati Reds games via satellite, in a room where he is surrounded by memorabilia sheathed in plastic—sells Avon and routinely gives you cologne and shampoo in bottles shaped like cowboys and footballs.

Your father's patients—ex-Olympians, ex-cons, masseuses, farmers, teachers, real estate agents, mechanics, bank tellers, prisoners in leg irons, drug addicts, mail carriers, covert marijuana farmers, pharmacists, overalled millionaires who own land-clearing companies—call him "Doc" or "Jim," pronouncing these words *Dawk* or *Jee-um*. You remember them and you don't. In the summer, they bring sacks of tomatoes and okra and corn and potatoes. Jars of honey. Venison jerky. Knives with pearlescent handles. Jellied rhubarb in jars with stickered lids that record dates of canning in scrawling cursive. There's Homer, a one-eared man who carries a bear vagina in his wallet. There's Monk, a raspy, baldheaded slab of a man who has a larynx that grinds words into hamburger. There's the wife of a pharmacist who owned for a brief period of time a gift store that sold sculptures of medieval villages. There's Kandi, the town poet and real estate agent, with whom you remember being enamored as a kid, partly because her name made you think of sweets and partly because a sheet of brunette hair fell down her back. There's Judy, the bank teller who's never been caught without makeup, not even when she mows her lawn or crawls in bed for the night. And there's Robert—a ruddy, big-cheeked, potbellied man who rides a moped and mows the office lawn, and who claims to be the cousin of Xavier Roberts, the inventor of the Cabbage Patch Kid Dolls. Robert has proposed on many occasions that he can get your family into Babyland General Hospital—in nearby Cleveland, Georgia—whenever you want. At Babyland General Hospital visitors can view a room where dolls emerge face first from the center of flaps of green fabric that have been sewn to resemble cabbages. The idea of a fake hospital intrigues you, but you hate dolls, especially these, with their squishy heads and adoption papers. You prefer Garbage Pail Kids, a cast of grotesque cartoon babies with names that seem lifted from some forbidden playground song: chubby-faced kids smoking cigarettes, barfing up blocks and live goldfish, crawling half-decomposed out of graves, wielding machine guns and sticks of dynamite, emerging from toilets. Garbage Pail Kids have names like Unzipped Zack, who unzips his face to reveal a grinning skull; Armpit Britt, a bikini'd gal proudly displaying yarn-thick tendrils of armpit hair; and Hy Gene, a lil' dude with a five o'clock shadow who razors a strip of flesh (it curls like a jagged apple peel) from his face. You probably shouldn't delight in these images—what would Jesus think?—but you do.

*

1985 is the Year of the Delorean, and of those twin infinity symbols that signify an exit out of the present, into the past, back to the future: 88. In 1985, the top NFL quarterbacks sport short-longs, and basketball players wear short-shorts. A white-bearded country singer is considered "hot." The hostage Terry Anderson is released. Johnny Carson jokes about the Ayatollah and Gorbachev. TVs advertise AT&T and Pepto and Metamucil and Grape-Nuts and Wrestlemania and Sanka and Beautyrest mattresses. Kids play Atari. Nancy Reagan consults a psychic. Women wear blazers and shoulder pads and bracelets that resemble gold CDs. The best NBA player is a dorky-looking white guy with a mustache. Mr. T plays a bad ass who's terrified to board a plane. Madonna's big eyebrows don't diminish her allure. Michael Jackson—his face sculpted but not yet grotesque—appears in magazines wearing aviator sunglasses, military-style jackets with epaulettes, and the white-sequined glove. He writes a song with Quincy Jones and sings it in a studio with a group of stars that includes Tina Turner, Bruce Springsteen, Willie Nelson, Billy Joel, Ray Charles, Smokey Robinson, Bette Midler, La Toya Jackson, Cyndi Lauper, Dionne Warwick, and Diana Ross. You hear this song on the radio of the carpool moms that allow rock music (in other words, everybody but yours). "We are the world," they sing, and though you and your friends think their earnestness is cheesy, you sing along with them.

If you thought about it, you'd have to admit: this is not a song you should be singing. You've been told—and more or less believe—that this world is not your home. That you're just passing through. Your treasures? Those are laid up beyond the blue. So it's not really right for you to lift your voice in unison with people who are saying that "we" are the "world."

What you believe: you are and you aren't.

*

Sometimes, after school you go home with the sisters—with Jolene and Raylene—to jump on their trampoline. One day somebody gets an idea: "Let's shout bad words while we bounce!" You won't remember what the sisters yelled because their words didn't make sense—they weren't words you knew. You only remember the word you yelled: the *S* word. Andrew Mintz—a tall, uncoordinated kid who took up most of the back seat during carpool—used to trick you into saying it, by asking you to say "it" after he said "sh." Raylene, though: she upped the ante. She yelled the *F* word. At the time, you had no idea what the *F* word meant. You'd never heard it before. As you jumped, leaping higher into the air, you yelled your respective bad words at the top of your lungs, as if they might help you fly. You yelled until your throats burned and your eyes watered. Then the sisters' mom—a joyful, freckly woman whose affection for other children was unappeasable and unabashed, a woman who used sliced veggie wieners as a pizza topping and let you crank up Air Supply and Kenny Loggins on the way to school and bought you soft serve cones at Micky D's afterwards—heard you and ordered everybody inside. The sisters went to their respective rooms, decorated with unicorn figurines, miniature Smurfs, and wicker basket seats that dangled from the ceiling. You sat in the living room, worried yourself sick while sitting at an ancient piano whose keys were chipped and yellow, like a set of bad teeth, listening to the sisters howl as their mom spanked them. Later, the mom came into the living room and softly said, "Do you know what that word means?"

You shrugged.

"Do you know what making love is?"

"Yes," you said, even though you didn't, just thought you did, thought you knew what love was, though if she'd pressed you and said, "No, not love, MAKING love," you would've faltered, not knowing love was something that could be made, could be manufactured, figured it occurred naturally, but she didn't press you, just said, "That's what the word means. It means when two people make love," which confused you, because you thought she'd been talking about the *S* word, and you'd always thought the *S* word was a word for defecation, a word your grandmother used, *defecate* for the *S* word and *void* or *micturate* for the *P* word. Later, your dad picked you up in his truck and took you home and on the way he told you the truth about how people were made. It flabbergasted you. You'd heard plenty about people in the Bible praying for children and then God giving them babies. You'd thought that was how it worked: a baby was the result of passing a test, having faith. And now you knew it was just like the older sister had told you, out by the rabbit cages: the male bunny sticks his penis in the female bunny, and a little while later baby bunnies come out.

*

On May 25th you will—finally, officially—be old enough to be baptized. It's a day you look forward to. You want to be a member of your church, which believes that the dead aren't really dead but merely sleeping, and that the rest of Christendom has forgotten the Fourth Commandment, which is "to remember the seventh day is the Sabbath of the Lord thy God," and that in the future the members of your church will be persecuted for not worshipping on Sunday, but that soon afterwards Jesus Christ will return and ferry those who have been steadfast to heaven. You want, during Communion Sabbaths, to make your younger sister envious by reaching for a thimble-sized glass of grape juice resting in a silver tray, to take a wedge of unleavened bread and chew it thoughtfully with your eyes closed. You are not, however, that crazy about participating in the Ordinance of Humility, during which you'll be called on to retrieve a towel and a silver basin of water, to wash the feet of another male parishioner. You pray that you'll be able to wash your father's feet. You'll peel his sock from his foot— an opaque, white appendage veined with blue—and slosh water between his toes, noting the patches of hair on the knuckles. You'll eyeball the lint sloshing in the basin. You'll thank God you don't have to wash the feet of other men, whose calves have been imprinted with elastic, and whose toenails are thick and yellow.

*

On Thursdays, a balding, mustachioed man—a pastor from Michigan who likes to listen to sad country music and calls ice cream cones "cones o' cream"—visits your home. Every week, in preparation for your baptism, you read and complete one of a series of blue booklets in a folder titled "Baptismal Study Guide." The series begins with a questionnaire titled "Spiritual Need Evaluation." It instructs the respondent— in this case, you—to read each question, then circle a letter between *A* and *E*, *A* signifying one's "highest interest" and *E* one's lowest. You circle *A*s for "Do you think Jesus will come in your lifetime?" and "Would you be embarrassed if you were asked to pray in a classroom?" and "Do you feel forgiven after you've prayed for forgiveness?" and "Does the Sabbath do anything positive in your life?" and "Do you enjoy the Sabbath?" and "Are you comfortable answering the question: Why are you a Seventh-day Adventist?" and "Do you feel that you are important to the church?" and "Do you feel that the Bible is a help to you in your daily living?" and "Do you understand what the Bible is saying about salvation?" and "Do you find the sermons you hear interesting and helpful?" and "Do you get anything out of going to church?" You circled *B*s for "Do you enjoy reading the Bible?" and "Do you read the counsel of Ellen White's books other than those required for classes?" and "Do you talk to your parents about spiritual things?" You circle a *C* for "Do you feel that prayer makes a difference in your life?" You circle no *D*s, but *E*s for "Have you read any of Ellen White's books other than those required for classes?" and "Do you talk to your friends about spiritual problems?"

The booklets tell stories: one relates the story about a man offering to take another man's punishment in a concentration camp. Another relates the story about a Papua New Guinea tribal chief who had a dream in which he was told to lead his people to another group of people who worshipped on the seventh day, and he did and now his entire village belongs to the Seventh-day Adventist church. A booklet titled "The Trinity" begins with a story about triplets. A "Think on This!" section asks readers to consider the "fact" that it takes more faith to believe in evolution than creation. The "Discussion and Reaction" part of "The Nature of Man" instructs the reader to "draw a simple picture of how you think you will look in your glorified, eternal condition, or list the things you would like to do in heaven as a first, second, and third choice." Yours are "Fly," "See God," and "Visit Space." In "The Great Controversy" booklet, you learn that "From the beginning of the conflict the entire universe has looked on with interest as Satan has made his charges against God." The "Jesus Christ" section begins with the story of an imposter Christ. In "The Remnant and Its Mission" discussion and reaction section, number 3 says, "I must be careful that I do not feel superior to other Christians because I have been given special understanding about the last special message for the world before Jesus comes. What are some of the ways we might feel superior, and how might I express them?"

You don't know how to answer this question.

You leave it blank.

*

In your father's office, you are summoned to examination rooms. His patients can't believe how much you've grown. They say things like, "He probably don't even remember me." And you don't. Not really. You feel known by people in the way the child of a celebrity might be known by the public: you—who exist largely within the private realms of church, church school, and your home—are often recognized but ultimately unknown.

Your father moves effortlessly among his fellow citizens: in hardware stores, pharmacies, supermarkets, gas stations, the post office, and barbershop. He buys chainsaw grease. Gloves. Kerosene. Coca-Cola in glass bottles. A haircut and neck shave from a six-foot-six barber named Jack, a WWII vet who isn't afraid to declare that he knows for a fact the Japanese have submarines parked beneath the city of Los Angeles.

Once a year he camps with a band of local men. They load jeeps and camper-topped Fords and Chevys with tents and sleeping bags and stoves and coolers of food and ascend to the tops of the highest ridges, where they hike balds of whispering mountain grass and gather blackberries in plastic pails. These men, like your father, boast thickly muscled hands. They do not work out. Aside from coon and dear and boar and turkey hunting, they play no sport. They don't give your father a hard time about his religion. They know when his church day is and respect him for having one. They dip fingers into Skoal tins and tobacco pouches. They spit into ribbed bottles or cans or between their feet as they rest elbows on their knees. They wear camouflage, overalls, mesh caps with the word *CAT* in yellow letters. They say "ain't never" and "they law" and "good Lord" and "shoot." They light cigarettes, blow smoke in dual plumes from their nostrils. Black lines rim their fingernails. One year somebody slides a *Playboy* into the sack of a man— tall, strong, overalled, head-quivering—who cannot read or write, can't sign his own name, who has never kissed or danced or held hands with a woman, and—from a distance—watch him turn the pages.

*

On your birthday, you stare into churning water: the waist-high pool where your body will be lowered and your spirit transformed. You know miles of this creek by heart; you can see it in your head. There's the pool where you caught your first fish using a line baited with a corn kernel, and there's where you took the butt end of a Buck knife and thwacked the head of a rainbow trout and held onto the slick, thrashing body, trying to avoid the sharp undersides of its scales. There's the falls where you've thrust your head, where the frigid roar took away your breath, causing you to remember how, according to your father, an overheated farmer had flung himself into a pool as cold as this and the subsequent shock stopped his heart. There's the giant boulders where you've surveyed the creek's most dangerous turn and where the water slows and deepens, lapping against a rock wall that bears—like an indecipherable inscription—a series of wavy lines indicating eons of water levels. There's the pool your dad threw you into when you'd sat on a yellowjacket's nest. There's the place where while he was chainsawing limbs you fell and broke your arm, and how at first he'd ignored you, because you cried when you fell into creeks, even when you didn't get hurt.

*

You don't believe baptism will save you—that is, you don't believe, as you know many people in your town do, that "once saved" means "always saved." Nobody in your church does. And yet: here you are. You are wearing a robe and tennis shoes as you wade into the stream. The water's frigid. But the pastor's not shivering. Behind him a froth of white bubbles. The pastor says the magic words—"I now baptize you in the name of the Father, the Son, and the

Holy Spirit"—and places a handkerchief over your mouth. He lowers you backwards into the stream. You go under; you rise up. A chorus of *Amens* follows. Church members sing. You're cold. The robe clings to your body. A fire blazes inside a makeshift pit your father built on a rock ledge. Sunlight flashes between cracks in rhododendron leaves. The people on the other side of the creek, the old women in folding chairs, the old men in their button-down shirts, your mother with her camera, your sister, your friends, are singing a hymn whose name or tune you won't remember. You'll know this is special, that nobody else has ever been baptized in this pool, but you don't feel any different. No shaft of light descends from heaven. No warmth floods your body. You know there are two of you: the you before the baptism and the you after. But aside from having experienced the event, you can't tell the difference. If you've been transformed, you can't feel it. You think maybe you're changed. That now you'll finish your Sabbath School lessons each week, that you'll be nicer to your sister. You hope you will. You worry you won't.

It—this nontransformation—is a secret that you keep from your father, whose eyes water when he stands before the pulpit as a deacon calling for the offertory, and from your mother, who plays piano with perfect posture, and from your sister, who fails to register, at least for now, as a person in whom you could ever confide, and from your uncle, who's a member of a famous Adventist singing group, and from your other uncle, who will one day become president of the world church, and from your grandmothers, one of whom you've never heard utter a harsh word about anyone and the other who worries that when she worries she's committing a grievous sin, and from your grandfathers, one of whom had been a beloved physician who had helped free a concentration camp during World War II and the other a dentist whose last three fingers on his left hand had been cut off, down to the first knuckle, by his older sister when he was three and she was six, who likes to think of himself, whenever he has occasion to ride a horse, as a cowboy. More significantly, it's a secret you keep from yourself, because you're afraid of what it might mean: that in the end you might not be who you say you are.

*

You'll get plenty of chances to pretend. Next year you attend summer camp—the "Tween" division, for twelve-year-olds—in the rolling hills of north Georgia. You use a bow to shoot arrows at targets pinned to haystacks in a hot, gnat-ridden field. You drop from a rope swing into a lake, line up for roll call, visit "Ma" and "Pa" at the Mountain Lore cabin, and watch Chad—a long-haired skateboarder—make out with Angela, the prettiest, tannest, blondest girl at camp. On Saturday you're sitting in church, a carpeted gymnasium, when at the end of the sermon a minister standing at a pulpit beneath a basketball goal asks the crowd—boys sitting on one side, girls on the other—a question: "Is there anyone here who wants to give their hearts to Jesus, to renew their lives for him? If so, would that person like to come forward, to the altar?" You hear the rustle of church bulletins, of dresses, of tennis shoes scuffing the gym carpet, but nobody rises—not at first. Not your friend Tom—a kid who wears Husky jeans and sleeps on hospital beds during his mom's night shifts at Murphy Medical—and not your friend Chris—a kid who lives with two brothers and a sister in a single-wide trailer on Hardscrabble Road in Mineral Bluff, Georgia, and who seems happiest when engaging in acts of subversion, flipping people the bird when no adults are looking, bragging about smoking rabbit tobacco. "Surely," the pastor says, his voice now booming through the microphone, "there's somebody who wants to rededicate his or her life. Surely there's somebody out there who feels compelled." Nobody rises. Not your friends. Not your enemies. Not the kid who brought the Guns N' Roses shirt. Not the kid who wears three pairs of striped athletic socks at once. Not Chad. Not Angela. The pastor calls again. And again. And still nothing. Nobody. You wonder how long he can go on. You fear you might be stuck here forever. You don't hear a voice saying *Go* or *Come* or *Now*. Even so, you rise from your chair. Your heartbeat works your blood into a coursing storm. You're shaking, but you walk down the aisle. You sense a stirring in the room. Every eye's focused on you. At the pulpit the pastor asks your name. You tell him, and he shouts it like an example: as if you're the embodiment of that which he'd been seeking. Another kid rises and comes forward. Others follow. Twos. Threes. Entire rows. A hundred preteens, illuminated by fluorescent lights, swarm forward. You fidget. You avoid their eyes, brimming now with sincerity, wonder if the ones who stay in their seats—including Tom and Chris—think you're a phony, and you wonder if now you'll have to act different. Be different. That people will expect more of you, and you won't know how to deliver. Most of all, you already feel guilty, because as much as you'd like to say that you did it for Jesus, your motivation was singular: to stop the calling. But don't admit that. Don't even think it. Tell yourself that God called you forward. Remind yourself that His eye is on the sparrow, and so how much more is it on you? One of the sisters from Happy Top winks at you; it's like you're a celebrity and a long-lost pal is employing a secret signal to say hello. The piano has started. You're all singing "Pass It On," the lyrics of which you'll never forget: "It only takes a spark, to get a fire going, and soon all those around, can warm up to its glowing. That's how it is with God's love." So true, you think, despite the fact that you've never told anyone about God's love—at least not anyone who didn't already know. But maybe you will. Maybe this is some kind of a turning point. You hope so. You won't want to be one of the ones who in the near future turns his face heavenward to watch as an everyday, run-of-the-mill cloud in the distance unscrolls to reveal itself as a mass of otherworldly fire and subsequently feel your eyeballs explode into flames. No. You'll want that light to bathe you like balm. Because that light won't be earthly fire: it'll be a spaceship made of angels and horses and rainbows and a throne upon which the Savior sits, the whole mass barreling toward the Earth like a massive vacuum cleaner, sucking the righteous dead from their graves and the righteous living from the cliffs and crags to which they'll be clinging, a stream of righteous souls gathering at the heart of a pulsing vessel, so as to escape the now-blazing pandemonium and fly somewhere far beyond the blue.

It's not only that you don't want to get burned alive with the rest of the wicked.

It's that everyone you love will be flying away forever.

And you don't want to get left behind.
You don't want to die.
So you sing.
Loud and clear.

> *Meet me in heaven.*
> *Pray that we all will be there.*

And here's the magical part: when you're singing, when your chest thrums with the reverberations, you have no doubts. The song is a sweetness, a foretaste of glory, a balm that allows you to feel—at least for the duration of the song—as if maybe the stories you've been told your whole life are true, and that now, today, you have been healed and made new.

NOTES FOR AN ESSAY ON SPECIAL MUSIC

> *Finally, brethren, whatsoever things are true,*
> *whatsoever things are honest, whatsoever things*
> *are just, whatsoever things are pure, whatsoever*
> *things are lovely, whatsoever things are of good*
> *report; if there be any virtue, and if there be any*
> *praise, think on these things.*
>
> —*Philippians 4:8*

Begin, maybe, with a description of Aunt Melinda, who was pretty and sweet but couldn't help herself from laughing at people in church when they sang, specifically those who were called upon—or who nominated themselves—to deliver "Special Music," which was a part of the service where a visitor or congregant came to the front of the church and, with or without accompaniment, sang. It wasn't ever supposed to be funny. Still, Aunt Melinda never failed to laugh. There was something about somebody standing in front of a group of church members and belting out a solo—or two people singing a duet, or three people singing in a trio, and so on—that she simply couldn't take. I was never sure why, but I figured that it had something to do with the idiosyncratic distortions that a face in midsinging often required—the raising of the eyebrows, the widening of the eyes, the stretching of the mouth. Then there were the sounds themselves: strained screeching, whining sopranos, thunderous baritones, off-key squelches. All of these elements conspired, in one way or another, to make Aunt Melinda laugh. She'd laugh if she averted her eyes. She'd laugh if she lowered her head. She'd clamp her mouth shut but her eyes would water. She'd try to suppress the laughing and in suppressing it begin to shake, to tremble, and then her entire pew would vibrate. Aunt Melinda was not malicious. She was not unkind. She simply couldn't help it. Laughing at singers was simply beyond her control.

*

Remind readers how the *special* in "Special Music" means "set apart." Significant. Esteemed. How it might be nice on some level to think that this was—or had been—an appropriately titled event. Sometimes it was. Sometimes it wasn't.

*

Explain how I came from a musical family? How my grandfather played the clarinet in a jazz band—albeit secretly, because it would disappoint his God-fearing parents, who certainly disapproved of the secular music and probably distrusted the transgressive nature of improvisation. How my Great-Aunt Dot—a jolly, chubby diabetic who kept Fruity Pebbles and chocolate mint ice cream bars in her kitchen—taught "Voice" for years at Southern Missionary College, in Collegedale, Tenn., where after she retired an auditorium was named in her honor. Maybe mention that LP of Aunt Dot we had, of her singing hymns in a quivery contralto? And the LP we owned of the band my Uncle Don played and sang with called the Wedgwood Trio, which some people joked was the Grateful Dead of Seventh-day Adventist bands. How my dad sometimes sat down and pounded out on our piano the one hymn he'd memorized, how he always sang bass during song service, and sometimes retrieved a trombone from a black case in our attic and blew low, lumbering melodies from its bell.

*

Then there was Mom. Who served as the pianist for her church—for forty years. Played hymns during song service. Played that little melody everybody sung quietly after the invocation. Accompanied anybody who was singing or playing an instrument for special music. Played for preludes and postludes. Practiced upcoming hymns at home every week. Rarely played simply for pleasure, or to pass the time, or to express herself, though she did play with precision and feeling. Rarely, if ever, missed a note. Knew a few classical songs by heart, would gladly sit down to play minuets and the like. But never played rock or pop or jazz or blues. Rarely played anything other than "sacred" music. Asked her once to help me play the theme song to the movie *Chariots of Fire,* and with her ears and hands and our record player she figured out the first few bars, wrote these notes on a blank sheet of music. Years later

I purchased the sheet music to a Hall and Oates song at a local music store. Couldn't make heads or tails of it. Too many sharps. Asked Mom for help. She tried to play the song. Failed. Then laughed. She, an accomplished pianist, could not for the life of her negotiate rhythm and blues. The more wrong notes she struck, the more she laughed.

*

Every day after school, my sister and I took turns practicing piano. Mom timed us with the oven clock. If we "messed around" or played anything other than our assigned music, she'd add minutes. I was lazy. Cheated by using visual memory and a half-decent ear. My piano teacher—a woman named Jennifer who ate candy bars during lessons and whose sleeveless dresses revealed the lurid flesh of her arms—played the notes and I watched her fingers and memorized patterns. This was easier than identifying notes, which seemed boring and lifeless and too often failed to reveal the secret of the music. Fingers, though. Fingers were alive and moving. Fingers I could trust. So I did.

*

Talk about how people who sang for "Special Music" in church were only sometimes actual musicians. My friend Raylene, whose nostrils flared when she sang, was not a musician. Elder Burke—a retired pastor, with slicked-back, jet-black hair, and a tiny mustache (the kind a maître d' at a French restaurant might wear)—was not a musician per se, but he sang voluminously and often made himself, simply by talking about how much he loved Jesus and wanted so badly to see him, cry. Sigmund, a diminutive German who sold a nutritional supplement called Barley Green—a vile-smelling powder that many Adventists in the 1980s stirred into glasses of water or juice and guzzled, sometimes pinching their noses, believing the beverage to have cancer-canceling properties—often treated church members to instrumentals on his violin, which he played with a stern and earnest passion. He seemed like a musician, sort of. He certainly seemed like he wanted people to think he was. He dedicated every song not to God but to his mother.

Anybody who wanted to perform "Special Music" could, as long as they had the desire. Which maybe made it not so "special" after all? Then again, who among our congregation would dare deprive another human soul of expressing oneself, through song, to God, in the public sphere of our church? As it turned out: nobody. Listeners might wish that the song would hurry up and finish itself. They might note that the particular arrangement did not sound pleasing to the ear. They might observe that the singer made weird faces or gesticulated or bobbed their heads or relied too heavily on vibrato. But there was nothing to do but wait until it was over and contribute to the hearty chorus of "Amens."

*

At some point, introduce Ellen G. White. Begin with the fact that she was a nineteenth-century prophetess who, with her husband, cofounded the Seventh-day Adventist church, to which nearly every person in my immediate and extended family belonged. At the age of nine Ellen had been walking home from school with her twin sister, when a classmate called her name. Ellen turned, and her classmate hurled—apparently for no other reason than meanness, though some said the act was inspired by Satan, who knew that God had already chosen Ellen as his messenger and wanted to interfere—a rock, which struck the prophetess-to-be squarely in the nose. Ellen spent the next three weeks unconscious. Though she would recover, she would remain ill for years and battle health problems for the remainder of her life. At nineteen, however, she experienced the first of what would henceforth be many visions, during which she would be shown a great many things about what human beings should shun, which included: butter, sugar, flesh food, secret vice, bicycles, novels, and photographs.

Of music, Mrs. White wrote that it "was made to serve a holy purpose, to lift the thoughts to that which is pure, noble, and elevating, and to awaken in the soul devotion and gratitude to God. What a contrast between the ancient custom and the uses to which music is now too often devoted! How many employ this gift to exalt self, instead of using it to glorify God! A love for music leads the unwary to unite with world lovers in pleasure gatherings where God has forbidden His children to go. Thus that which is a great blessing when rightly used, becomes one of the most successful agencies by which Satan allures the mind from duty and from the contemplation of eternal things."

*

I remembered hearing—or having heard, at some point—that the melodies of many of the beloved hymns we sang had originated as songs sung in bars, by drunks. Was this true? Apparently not. According to the Internet, John Wesley and Martin Luther did not appropriate the melodies of "drinking songs" in order to write their hymns. Then again, William Booth, founder of the Salvation Army, did. According to Helen Hosier, who wrote *William and Catherine Booth: Founders of the Salvation Army*, Booth's argument was simple: "Why should the devil have all the best tunes?"

*

Explain how as a kid I'd been taught that every possible human experience should be subject to close—if not microscopic—scrutiny, and that products of this world— songs, T-shirts, books, movies, magazines, TV shows, and amusements of any kind—might and very well *could* be spring-loaded booby traps laid by the Devil. So deeply had this idea been embedded, it'd become hard-wired in my brain. I'd hear a song and immediately pass judgment, thinking, *Oh, that's bad!* I knew singing about something served to elevate it. All singing, then, was a form of worship. Sing about something sad, sing about something earthly, and you just might be singing something Satanic.

Another danger? You would become like whatever it was that you exposed yourself to; for instance, if you listened to too much Metallica, you might grow your hair long and start bellowing things like, "Our brains are on fire / with the feeling to kill / And it won't go away / until our dreams are fulfilled."

*

Sometimes, though, I'd hear a song and think, *That's bad* and *I like it.* And then, with a certain hopefulness, *But maybe it's not that bad?*

*

Of loud, brash singing, Ellen White wrote, in *Selected Messages, Book 2,* "the Holy Spirit never reveals itself ... in such a bedlam of noise. This is an invention of Satan to cover up his ingenious methods for making of none effect the pure, sincere, elevating, ennobling, sanctifying truth for this time.... A bedlam of noise shocks the senses and perverts that which if conducted aright might be a blessing."

*

Rewind to May 5, 1985. I'm sitting with a tape deck and old clock radio in the sun porch of our house: a sixteen-windowed room that allowed a 180-degree view of the rhododendron grove in the cove at the base of a mountain where we lived. The clock part of the radio was analog: that is, it had an hour and minute and second hand. It had a tuner—a little wand that slid along a row of numbers. I turned the dial, scrolling through static until I found a station that happened to be playing Casey Kasem's *Top Forty.* Can't remember why—maybe because I wasn't allowed to purchase popular music—but I decided to press the record button on the tape deck. The number-one song that week was "White Horse," an electro/synth-pop/post-disco number by a Danish band named Laid Back. Even now, when I hear those fuzzy, stuttering beats and that loping bass, I return to that day when I lay mesmerized on a carpet checkered with dark and light green squares. Where had my parents gone? Were they outside gardening? Mowing the lawn? The only thing that mattered: they weren't there to stop me.

*

How did I pay for the first cassette tapes I ordered using my Columbia House membership, which promised twelve albums for the price of a penny—not including, of course, "shipping and handling"? Can't remember. Must have written a check. At fourteen? Did I have a checking account then? Maybe. First batch of tapes included Whitney Houston, New Kids on the Block, Duran Duran, The Cure, R.E.M., Terence Trent D'Arby, George Michael, Information Society, DJ Jazzy Jeff & The Fresh Prince. Remember lining up the cases so that all the labels faced me and I could therefore admire them. How I stared at them thinking, *These are my tapes.* Savoring the sense of ownership. Feeling validated. That in the end I was a person who had actual tapes. Tapes were cool. Was I cool? Might I be? I hoped so, maybe. But only unless it didn't mean I didn't end up like the people who, in one of Mrs. White's first visions, were traveling along a narrow pathway of light, took their eyes off the Savior, fell into the darkness below, and never came back.

*

Talk about MTV. How at the house in the shadowy cove where my family lived we didn't have cable—the lines didn't run out that far. So no MTV. Therefore, whenever I encountered the channel, my eyes glazed over. Discuss vivid memory of standing in the master bedroom of a couple who were my parents' friends—Ellen and Leon—and how the video to Michael Jackson's "Beat It" appeared onscreen. Those initial notes: synth-gongs signaling something ominous. The howling ruffians leaping off a loading dock. The manhole cover sliding open. The white dude with the feathery hair and a toothpick dangling from his mouth. Michael Jackson on a bed, hugging a pillow, emerging later in that red leather jacket. The dance fighting. How even though Michael was, like me, boyish and fragile looking, he'd mastered his body in a way that was inexplicable. I, on the other hand, had not. No matter how often I tried to use the reflection of the glass windows of our church to see myself moonwalk, I never quite mastered MJ's fluid effortlessness.

*

Note this, at some point: the vast majority of Seventh-day Adventists do not dance. They don't slow dance. They don't square dance. They don't waltz, clog, or salsa. As Mrs. White said, "The true Christian will not desire to enter any place of amusement or engage in any diversion upon which he cannot ask the blessing of God. He will not be found at the theater, the billiard hall, or the bowling saloon. He will not unite with the gay waltzers, or indulge in any other bewitching pleasure that will banish Christ from the mind." But Adventists do—or did—"march." Our church held socials in the fellowship hall where people marched in unison to rousing band music blasted from a portable tape deck. Our leader was the aforementioned Elder

Burke, the one with the pencil-thin mustache and head of jet-black hair, who cried when he talked about longing to see the face of Jesus. While he marched, Elder B. might have carried a baton. At any rate, he was a vociferous and jubilant leader—one we all eagerly followed.

*

Not once have I ever seen my parents dance together. The only members of my family on both sides who ever danced earnestly were Effie and Luther, my now-dead great-uncle and great-aunt. They lived in Greenville, South Carolina, in a little brick house across the great big field that separated their home from my grandparents' place. For years, Luther sold vegetables out of a van. Then he went to bed for ten years. Had a hernia, and his particular condition had allowed his intestines to end up inside of his ball sack, which my father had once seen and said was—as improbable as this sounds—as big as a basketball. When Luther wasn't in bed, he was a silly old man, one who repeated the same half-dozen lewd jokes he knew and afterwards laughed hilariously, which would always prompt Effie to swat him with the back of her hand or a dish towel and say, "Luther! NOBODY wants to hear ANY of that." On Christmas Day, before Luther retreated to bed for a decade, we would walk from my grandparents' house and across the field to Effie and Luther's to eat roast beef and biscuits. Luther would open the lid of a cabinet in the living room and place a record—"Jingle Bell Rock"—on a turntable. Then he and Effie would dance. Impressively so for their ages, or so I always thought. They had rhythm.

Luther would spin Effie around. Their hips would swing. Everyone would laugh and clap. This kind of dancing—to a Christmas song whose "rock and roll" seemed comparably quaint when compared to the heavy beats and suggestive nature of contemporary music—seemed acceptable in everybody's eyes. But nobody else joined in.

*

How dad wouldn't look when Mom danced. I had to agree: it wasn't pretty. It was, in fact, a parody of dancing that had over the years become a parody of itself, as if my mother was celebrating her refusal to take dancing seriously. She bit her lip. She snapped her fingers. She gyrated. Dad shielded his eyes with a hand. Mom put her hands on her hips and said, "You don't like to watch me dance?" Dad would say simply, "No, I don't." And Mom would laugh hysterically.

*

Explain how, at the Seventh-day Adventist boarding school I attended as a teenager, students weren't allowed to have radios or 8-tracks or tapes or CD players. Somebody once got in trouble for using a U2 song during the end-of-the-year slideshow. But students could play Bonnie Tyler's "Total Eclipse of the Heart," as long as it was being used as the soundtrack to the antidrug skit our school performed at least once a year—a didactic, pantomimed melodrama about a boy, who after engaging in a heated fight with his father, leaves home and is soon embraced by a group of teens wearing all black and who take the cardboard signs hanging from their necks—each Sharpied with various drug names, like "PCP," "ANGEL DUST," "WEED," "COKE," and "SNUFF"—and transfer them to the neck of the boy and then clasp their hands together and form a circle around him, which the father and the boy attempt to break through but can't, at least not until they both fall to their knees in prayer, at the exact moment when "Total Eclipse of the Heart" reaches its dramatic crescendo. And then the circle of students collapses, and the father and son embrace.

*

How certain kids at my boarding school—my roommate Scott, for instance, who used to stare at himself in the mirror with pursed lips and growl about how he looked just like Simon Le Bon—got to a point where they felt so guilty about their music consumption that they burned entire tape collections. I remember someone saying that they could hear screams—they were faint, but definitely audible—as the cassettes melted. The spirits of demons, maybe, that had once possessed the music, now fleeing the flames. Or just the whistle of air through holes in burning plastic.

*

How, if my mom came to pick me up for home leave or an open weekend at my boarding school, I'd play a mixtape featuring rock songs I'd learned, through trial and error, that she wouldn't complain about. I always included The Cure's "Just Like Heaven," because I'd played it before in her presence and never heard her say, "What in the world is this?" or "This is about to drive me crazy," or "I can't hear anything but drums." She never actually came out and said that drums were in and of themselves *evil*, but I figured this was what she probably believed, didn't even want to ask for fear of hearing that, yes, drums were bad, had demon-summoning powers, could put you in a trance, could mesmerize, and one who is mesmerized is one who is not in control of one's mind, and if one isn't in total control of one's mind, then who is? The answer being of course probably, maybe, actually—Satan. But what if you just liked the *sound* of a song? Just liked the way it sounded? And what if this song, say, was a love song? Love songs were nice, right? Love came from God, didn't it? Technically, yes, but you also had to ask, as always, what the singer was striving to glorify. It was a question I avoided asking myself, back when I was fifteen and enamored with The Cure, and with the band's lead singer and songwriter, a pale, mascara-and-smeared-lipstick–wearing chap who sported a haystack hairdo—an artfully disheveled mop of dyed black hair that looked not unlike he'd been electrocuted—and who wore big black baggy sweaters and black jeans and giant white high top sneakers and whose stage presence was not unlike an awkward nine-year-old girl who wanted to dance but was too shy. The Cure played dark, dirge-y funereal music. They played shamelessly upbeat pop songs. But they also had songs with lyrics like, "I'll nail you to the floor and push your guts all inside ow-how-out" and had albums with song titles like "Pornography," "Torture" and "The Snakepit" and "Screw" and, most problematically, "The Blood," a track from the album *Head on the Door* that featured flamenco-style acoustic guitar, a song that I forced myself to skip when I played the CD, despite how cool that rollicking guitar sounded, because it contained the lyrics "I am paralyzed by the blood of Christ / though it clouds my eyes / I can never stop." Though I had no way of knowing that the song was actually about an alcoholic beverage called the "Tears of Christ," I worried that this was The Cure's official take on the actual blood of Christ, that it contained paralyzing properties, a theory that seemed at odds with what I'd been taught, and which I believed: that the blood of Christ washed away my sins.

*

As a senior in boarding school I discovered the first and longest letter my father had ever written to me—a letter I read once and never saw again because he never actually delivered it and, I presume, threw it away. This was back when I'd first taken to borrowing my father's clothes— especially his old flannel shirts—proudly thinking, *I'm as big as Dad now.* I'd been rummaging through his sweaters in a dresser drawer when I found a folded stack of notebook paper: I remember it was lined and light blue and that each page was just a little bigger than the palm of my hand. I don't remember how the letter started, whether he said "Dear Son" or used my name in the salutation, only how strange it was to see so much of his handwriting in one place at once. I'd always admired his signature, thought his handwriting looked better than my mother's, which was a bubbling hodgepodge of cursive and print, a fact that never made much sense to me because she was the artist, she was the one who could paint and sew and draw. By this point in my life, my mother had written me volumes: daily notes in my elementary school lunchbox, cards on holidays and birthdays, weekly letters sent to my boarding school mailbox, the envelope flaps decorated with stickers she saved especially to decorate her correspondence. If my father, who preferred real-time conversation, had ever written so much as a single phrase on so much as a birthday card, I couldn't remember. And yet here in my hands were pages of words and sentences, all addressed to me. I can't remember if the letter was complete, since it would make sense for an unfinished letter to remain unsent, nor can I remember any one line in particular, only that the gist of it was that my father had seen a stack of CDs in my room, and out of curiosity had looked through them, and what he'd seen had troubled him. He didn't know much about rock music, didn't listen to or keep up with any contemporary secular music that I knew of, and preferred, when listening to the radio, to listen to old-time gospel, or to preachers who sermonized with great, gasping fervor. But he knew about Guns N' Roses. He said he'd known I listened to rock music but hadn't guessed that my tastes ran so dark. Can't remember much about the letter, except that it composed a thoughtful kind of admonishment, expressed anxiety about that darkness seeping into my life, and if it was true that there was nothing more important than a relationship with Christ, he couldn't see how Axl Rose fit into the equation. And though I couldn't articulate a valid response, years later I asked him about the letter and why he'd never sent it. He said he didn't know. That it wasn't the only letter he'd written to me. That maybe, in the end, he'd written those letters more for his own sake than for mine.

*

Was I really supposed to only listen to sacred music? It wasn't that I disliked it. I loved the album *Angel Band* by Emmylou Harris. I loved to belt out "Blessed Assurance." I loved the song "Borrowed Angel," by the Anita Kerr Choir, which my father put on the hi-fi on Friday nights, as the sun was going down, and whose velvety harmonies helped us welcome the Sabbath hours. Even so, didn't the writer of Ecclesiastes say, "There was a time for everything"? Didn't that contradict Paul's instruction to "be joyful always"? Was such a thing as being "joyful always" even possible? What kind of preternaturally gifted human could praise God in *all* circumstances? Sure, Job had done it, but he was, like, the best of the best, and God had known that from the beginning, which was why he gave Satan permission to drain the man's wealth and kill all ten of his children plus his servants, and to afflict him with boils. God knew Job would praise him no matter what. And he did. And so was rewarded in the end.

*

One thing I couldn't deny, and never did: singing was always the best part of worship. For instance, on Friday nights, after vespers at my boarding school, our chaplain would announce that anybody who wanted to sing could stay for a while afterwards. After a group of us convened, our chaplain would lead us outside into the night. We'd follow the bobbing blob of his flashlight as we walked down Academy Drive—the strip of unmarked asphalt that wound from Reeves Station Road to our school—and then we'd stand at the sign that bore our school's name. There, we formed a circle, and if we were lucky we got to hold the hand of someone we liked, perhaps even adored, and our chaplain would ask us what we wanted to sing, and someone would shout out the title of a song, and then someone else would start us off, maybe too high at first and someone else would suggest a lower key, and we'd start again. I always hoped we'd sing "Pass It On," and we always would. "Meet me in heaven," we'd sing, "we'll hold hands together." And there, under the stars, next to my friends, my chest would swell, and the song would help me believe—at least for a little while—that such a thing just might be possible.

HOW TO WRITE A LOVE STORY

Begin, at fourteen, by shipping off to a Seventh-day Adventist boarding school in the sweltering foothills of the Blue Ridge Mountains. Endure three years of dorm life: wedgies and wrestling matches and random room searches and, thanks to whatever dickhole slathered your boxer briefs—every last one—with handfuls of IcyHot, a scorched scrotal sac. Walk every morning through the dark, to the chapel. Sing praise songs. Make selections from a heartbreakingly dismal cafeteria menu, which, thanks to the health-conscious nineteenth-century prophetess who cofounded your denomination, is unabashedly vegetarian and serves an endless variety of meat-shaped, gravy-drenched soy products. Shower beneath the prickling rays of nozzles protruding from a single chrome column in a tiled room—with as many as five other dudes. On the rare occasion that you find an empty bathroom, beat off in a locked stall; spend the rest of the day worrying about the fact that you did that thing you promised God you'd never do again—*again*. Wonder if this time you'll have finally reached your forgiveness quota, and that, at the End of Time, God will play a movie of you pulling your pud on a giant screen suspended in space, to help explain to your loved ones—and the rest of the Redeemed—why you didn't make it to heaven. Hope it's not too late to change course. Remind yourself about the time Jesus refused to condemn that adulterous woman and then told her to "go and sin no more." Rededicate yourself. Promise to love your neighbors. Sing songs about meeting them all in heaven, while secretly hoping Jesus might delay His coming a little longer, so that before you're ferried away to a sexless eternal paradise, you'll get a chance to kiss a girl, put your hand up her shirt, date her, get engaged, and fuck your brains out in the blissful confines of holy matrimony. Finally bust a move on a girl—the granddaughter, as it turns out, of a famous Adventist televangelist—only to discover that, from what you can tell, she shaves—but apparently without the requisite care—her upper lip. Two weeks later, dump her for a girl who lives off campus, a girl who wears Liz Claiborne pantsuits and drives a gold Fiero and whose hot blonde mom signs you out of the dorm on Saturday afternoons so that—liberated from the oppressive rules of your school, which maintains a strict "hands-off" policy— you and your new squeeze can enjoy make-out sessions in the privacy of her Ralph Lauren–themed bedroom. Spend Sunday afternoons listening to a contraband Walkman and teaching yourself to play the epic solo from that one super-long song on Jane's Addiction's *Ritual de lo Habitual*. Wonder if any—if not all—of the musicians you love are secret Satan worshippers; console yourself with the notion that their pentagrams and eye shadow and black lipstick are best understood as a series of ironically employed theatrics, deployed to unsettle those who cherish the safe but utterly banal rituals of society's conventions, or whatever. Grow out your hair—long enough for your dean to demand that you cut it. Ignore him. Haze some freshmen, because your friends, as Resident Assistants, have master keys, and because that Jamie kid had it coming, had practically earned, by running his big fat mouth, the trash bag full of water you threw onto his sleeping body, and because, shit, you got hazed ten times as hard when you were his age.

Six months after Fiero girl gives you the boot, set your sights on the unattainable: the hot Korean girl who's never had a boyfriend. The one whose wardrobe includes a mustard-colored blouse, a pair of billowing purple pantaloons, and a gold, chain-link belt: an ensemble that embellishes whatever mystique she's already cultivated, what with that long black hair licking the curve of her ass, the mischievous gleam in her eyes, and her inexplicable flexibility, which allows her during gymnastic exhibitions to hook her feet behind her head and roll her body—now a circle—across blue padded mats. The one who flirts relentlessly with any boy who gives her a hard time, as if she were playing a game she was desperate to win, who practically lives in order to be pestered or argued with, and appears to love nothing more than being challenged by the opposite sex, if only so that she could prove in the end that she's superior, simply because she's a girl. The one we'll call—and why not?—Eve.

You're no stranger to Eve's gleeful aggression. During Pony Express—the Sunday night ritual where boys and girls exchange handwritten letters—she'd send you a scrap of notebook paper, on which she'd scrawl the last word in a heated dispute about how Koreans were a superior race, or how guys were pigs, or how Dominique Wilkins would— given the chance—annihilate Michael Jordan in a game of one-on-one, closing the dispatch with "Your friend," then her name, followed by ellipses, then "The Bitch." On the basketball court—the one place where boys could feel like champions (even though competition outside of intramurals was not allowed, since the prophetess had decreed, more or less, that a competitive nature could poison one's spiritual life by emphasizing earthly rather than heavenly rewards)— she often sat cross-legged on the stage of the gym, cupping her hands over her mouth to better direct her insults, which only made you play harder and wrinkle your nose and point at her on the rare occasions you drained a three.

But seriously, why *not* go for gold? It's your senior year. Time to make your mark, accomplish something significant. And anyway, haven't you've always sort of liked her? Haven't you always admired how pretty and smart and intimidating she is? How there's something extra hot about a fine girl with a ruthless sense of humor, one who specializes in quick-witted mockery? You just haven't had the chance to really get to know her—much less the guts to make a move. Not that she'd ever let you. Which somehow deepens her mystique. She may be smarter than you, but you have a sense that underneath the layers of complicated defense mechanisms she's got a regular human heart, vulnerable as any other, maybe more so. Which explains the tough outer shell: it's terrified of getting broken.

*

In the beginning, keep it simple. Sit at Eve's table in the cafeteria. Make her laugh by doing impersonations of faculty: the Industrial Arts teacher who purses his lips when describing the "gnurling" of pistons; the Chemistry teacher who resembles one of those fat, bespectacled nerds in *The Far Side*. Convince her to partner with you for that stupid project Pastor Cook assigns every year to seniors in his Bible class, the one where everyone has to plan a fake wedding—followed by the creation of a fake family budget and a fake search for a fake home—in order to demonstrate just how time-consuming and expensive and complicated these future events will be, as if imagining the attendant fiscal challenges of a church-sanctioned union will prevent young people from rushing into marriage.

But whatever you do—whether you're copying answers from her German workbook or applauding her ability to eat a burrito that's been drowned in twenty packets of hot sauce—don't come on too strong. Don't spook Eve with declarations or romantic overtures. Be patient. Imagine each interaction as a deposit on an investment, one whose maturation will result in nothing less than taking full possession of that oh-so-vulnerable heart.

*

Like all students at Georgia–Cumberland Academy, you have to work, but that doesn't mean your job has to suck. Avoid employment that requires you to stir stainless steel vats of veggie-meat casserole. Avoid lawn mowing and flowerbed weeding and toilet scrubbing. And, for the love of all that's holy, don't sew cushions for lawn chairs at the small factory at the edge of campus. Instead, land the cushiest job possible: night monitor for the boys' dorm front desk. This way, you can do what every other student does between the hours of seven and ten p.m.—study, stare into space, talk about girls—*and* get paid for it. Sure, occasionally you'll need to vacuum the lobby or Windex the windows or retrieve the person for whom one of the dorm's three pay phones rings, but mostly you eavesdrop on those phone conversations or shoot the shit with the Assistant Boys' Dean—a lanky, laid-back Californian named Ken—or the Assistant Chaplain—a self-proclaimed surfer dude who once engineered the auto-reverse feature of a confiscated Walkman so that it could play "Stairway to Heaven" backwards, so as to provide irrefutable evidence that Robert Plant does indeed call the devil "my sweet Satan."

As an R.A. for the girls' dorm's freshman hall, Eve also works at night. This, friend, is *key*. Since you both finish classes by noon, your afternoons are wide open. Relax while your fellow students wolf down their platters of spaghetti or lentil loaf: you don't have anywhere to be for, like, six hours, until after rec period. Sculpt leftover mashed potatoes into a pyramid and think of ways to keep Eve occupied. Propose a round of Muk-jji-ppa (a faster, frantic, Korean version of Rock, Paper, Scissors). Ask her to teach you how to curse in her native tongue, or practice dialogues for German class. And when the kitchen staff finally boots you out, plop down outside in the sun-singed grass of central campus. Build tiny sailboats out of stray magnolia leaves. Compete for who can pluck the most four-leaf clovers. But most importantly? *Talk.* Discuss everything you can think of: God, love, death, college, parents, and what it'll be like to escape this epic shithole where your every move is being constantly monitored. Congratulate yourself when Eve admits that she doesn't think—although she once did—that you're a total space case. But don't get your hopes up. She knows boys only want one thing—a body—whereas she's interested in the opposite—a *mind*. Argue with her about this. Lie if you have to. Wear her down. Compliment her. Inch closer. Help her look for split ends. Rest an arm on her shoulder. Hug her tight and hard during the single goodnight hug that boys and girls are allowed to exchange. Relish every millisecond of physical contact, but for the love of God keep your mouth shut about it. The last thing you want to do is to remind her that she has an anti-boyfriend force field, and that you're working—ever so diligently—on the deactivation code.

*

Recognize this: Georgia–Cumberland Academy has a shit ton of rules. For one thing, it's got an insurance agency breathing down its neck, something your dean reminds you every time you complain about being confined to campus. Furthermore, as a Christian institution, the school has a responsibility to train students in the ways they should go. This means no rock music. No radios. No TV. No Dungeons & Dragons. No role-playing games, period. No jewelry (not even so-called "friendship bracelets"). No cussing. No alcohol or tobacco. Not even any caffeine (though if you're desperate, there's a guy on sophomore hall who sells warm, black-market Coca-Colas for a buck, out of a suitcase in his closet). No prolonged physical contact with the opposite sex. And no dancing. Bodies gyrating to drumbeats? Too pagan. Too primal. And too overtly sexual. It's like your math teacher—a guy with gray hair and an unshaven philtrum and plaid button-ups and an honest-to-God pocket protector, a guy who, to get a laugh while he's standing in the cafeteria line, will flip his dentures in and out with his tongue—says, "You can't dance until you're married, and then you can dance with your hands in your wife's pants," a garish little rhyme that you find odd, partly because his partner—a dainty little witch of a woman with a mane of unkempt hair—only wears ankle-length dresses.

Bottom line: Georgia–Cumberland Academy students aren't allowed to dance, so they don't go to dances, balls, or proms. They go to *banquets*. And banquets, as it turns out, are a huge fucking deal. Sometimes guys ask girls. Sometimes girls ask guys. Sometimes there's drama—like that time during freshman year you asked out the scorching-hot junior who worked in the chaplain's office and wore boots with Guess jeans and red lipstick and had a sultry face with hooded eyes, and she said yes to you and no to Sean, a pompous sophomore with a shark fin nose he seemed to keep—at all times—slightly raised, and the next day all your friends congratulated you. Sometimes the banquets have themes, like "safari" or "county fair." Sometimes they're fancy—guys with boutonnières pinned to the lapels of rented tuxedos, girls with corsages pinned to the shoulder straps of frilly-skirted dresses, the hemlines of which must be dean-approved. Sometimes you board buses and head to local hotel conference rooms and eat vegetarian lasagna and salad and cheesecake from segmented Styrofoam platters. If you're lucky, there'll be a movie, something benign and lame like *The Scarlet Pimpernel,* which means the lights will be dimmed and you'll get to surreptitiously grip the hand of your date, rubbing your thumb over hers with purpose and urgency. And if you're *really* super lucky—if it's dark outside by the time you head back to campus and your faculty chaperone lets you sit with your date and the driver doesn't drive with the interior bus lights on—you just might get to suck some face.

This year's first banquet, the one where you ask Eve and she says yes, writing her response on the inside of a folded piece of foil from a Hershey bar wrapper, is sorta— but not totally—lame. The student association—of which Eve had been elected president at the end of the previous year, an odd move for a person who was so antagonistic that she seemed to relish the fact that people thought she was a bitch—hasn't raised enough money to fund an off-campus excursion. So they hold a '50s-themed banquet in the cafeteria, a drab place whose carpet is stained and whose ceiling preserves squiggles of dried spaghetti noodles, flung there by mischievous dorks of yore.

To prepare: slick your hair back, roll a box of candy cigarettes you bought at Walmart during last week's town trip inside a T-shirt sleeve. Admire Eve in her poodle skirt, her hair ponytailed with a scarf. Play guitar while your roommate, a spiky-haired blond with fat arms and tiny protrusions on his T-shirt thanks to his permanently erect nips, croons the lyrics for "Earth Angel," a song that's quaint enough to meet faculty approval. Take pictures with your arm around Eve—a totally sanctioned boy-touching-girl situation because it's quick and casual. Tack these photos to the corkboard above the desk in your dorm room. Stare at her smiling face for long periods of time. Feel your pulse quicken. Let yourself think, *She could be it. Like, the* one.

*

Stop caring—as if you ever really did—about academics. Roll your eyes when anybody mentions college applications, since it's common knowledge that the only thing an Adventist kid has to do to get into a denomination-sponsored college is to produce fog on the surface of a mirror. Give zero shits about chemistry: a C- means, "Dude, you passed." Choose—randomly and without a second thought—the stocks you'll pretend to invest in during Economics class. Refuse to join the students who are protesting the principal's decision to ban Shakespeare from Senior English, after three students—not the brightest, but certainly the most "outwardly religious"—refused to read *Macbeth* because of its depiction of witchcraft, and after your teacher—a white-haired old woman who'd sunbathed herself into a mass of animated wrinkles—assigned them *Paradise Lost*, which they also snubbed, because by imagining Satan's point of view they might be tempted to sympathize with his plight.

Spending less time on schoolwork means more time to think about Eve, more opportunities to scribble notes, draw pictures, and write poems. Do anything for her; in fact, do everything *because* of her. If she gets jealous of your other friends who are girls—and she will—pledge to ignore them forever. The Chinese girl who plays tennis and piano who's been your friend for three years? Eve knows that you guys had a thing once, even though it never really was a thing. So stop writing her letters. The blonde with braces, the one who enthusiastically leads song service, the one who taught the student body a bunch of songs from the antidrug conference she attended? Eve knows she likes you, or used to like you, or once said you were cute, so smile or wave at your peril.

Oh, and this is important: overanalyze *everything*. When you enter the cafeteria, and Eve, sliding her tray toward the juice machine, doesn't immediately see you and smile, panic. Is she ignoring you on purpose? Or is she only pretending to ignore you so that you won't think she's too into you? Is this a pride thing? Has she overcommitted to the urge to produce that impression? There's no way to know. In chapel, glance over your shoulder, see her holding a clipboard, placing checks next to the girls' names on her hall. Is that feigned or real absorption, from which she emerges—but for only a second—to give you a brief smile and wave before returning to what seems to be, by the look of her furrowed brow, a serious enterprise that involves nothing less than her total and complete concentration? You have no idea. And you worry you never will.

*

Though pursuing Eve isn't always fun, it does involve games. Just when you think you're making progress, she'll claim that this whole thing between you guys—your friendship, your "relationship," whatever name you want to give to it—has been one big joke, and that she only wanted to see if she could actually get you to fall for her, and that she was only interested in teaching you that girls couldn't be trusted, and that she could never really love you, because really, are you that arrogant? Did you think you had that kind of power? Tell yourself, when she laughs in your face then whips around and runs back to her dorm, that you know she doesn't mean it, but worry that maybe she wanted to. Return to your own dorm, eyes stinging, faint with nausea, as if her words—like a series of well-handled knives—had penetrated your body, had hollowed it out.

Catch up to her after supper—macaroni with peas, wedges of mushy casserole, whole-wheat buns clutching veggie wieners—and say things like, "You can't do this" or "This isn't fair." Reinvigorate your nausea when you hear the sound of your plaintive voice. Brace yourself against the cafeteria's brick exterior. Warn her that you're going to be sick. This, as it turns out, is an effective method. She grabs you by the arm, whispers, "Don't you dare, don't you *dare* throw up."

How, she wants to know, could you ever have doubted her? You are, she reminds you, the only person in whom she's ever truly confided. You have pages of evidence to prove this—letters that say things like, *please don't have a stomachache ever again* and *someday you will find a girl who can love you better than me* and *forget about me* and *don't forget about me!* and *the only way to get rid of me is to tell me to leave and never talk to you again* and *I guess I just like trouble and want to avoid the sickening feeling of true love* and *to always be happy is not a sign of a strong relationship* and *no one's ever happy unless they're dead, I learned that in Bible class* and *hold me and make my demons leave.*

And Eve does have demons. As far as you can tell, they were gifted to her by her parents, who want the fruit of her womb to be pure, and whose heads, when they imagine freckled grandchildren, go absolutely fucking bananas. Not that your own family is thrilled by the idea of your dating a person of another race, which is why, you suppose, that when you tell your dad about Eve, he says that Asian women "don't age well," and that your grandmother, upon seeing Eve's school pictures, says, without skipping a single beat, "Koreans ... Now aren't they supposed to be the ugliest of the Asians?" The thing is, even if Eve's parents could conceive of "American boyfriend" as a temporary concept, they've promised swift retribution if she should ever marry a white boy: they will straight-up *disown* her. So with these future obstacles to consider, come up with plans: four years for college, four more to become totally financially independent, and bam, in eight years you'll both be free.

*

In January, Eve delivers a troubling confession: she doesn't like kissing. She hadn't kissed anybody before New Year's Eve, when during winter break you obtained permission from your parents to drive to Atlanta to hang at your friend Ed's house, which you did, for a couple of hours, before switching venues to a cheap downtown hotel room where some of your more enterprising friends had pooled their resources to obtain a bottle of vodka, a dime bag of weed, and a pack of Benson & Hedges. Ignore the vodka and weed and cigarettes—you and Eve are still pretending, mostly for the benefit of the other, that your bodies, as temples of God, shouldn't be sullied by the poisons of drugs. And anyway, you didn't come here to get fucked up. You came to be alone with Eve. So persuade her at some point to take a walk. Once you're out of sight of everybody else, plant one on her.

Poor technique? Too much tongue? Bad breath? You don't know, and Eve won't explain what, if anything, you did wrong. Instead, she claims your past history's the problem: in other words, the fact that you've kissed girls who weren't her. Eve refers to these girls, who were both white and blonde, as "your dumb blondes." It doesn't matter that neither of them attends your school any longer. The thought of your mouth on theirs makes Eve want to barf. You might even still have their germs! Wonder if she's joking—or simply insane. Entertain what feels like a very real possibility: Eve will never kiss you again. Considering that you have a pretty strong fondness for kissing, this is highly problematic, especially if it turns out that she's the one you want to be with until the end of time.

Let your heart be not troubled. What you don't know—not yet—is that Eve is just as horny as you, and as soon as she learns how to shut off her brain and swallow her pride, you'll be better than fine. See Exhibit 1: the night the seniors beat the juniors at the annual junior/senior basketball game. To celebrate, board, with the rest of your class, a bus headed for Pizza Hut. Sit next to Eve—she's so proud of you! You scored the most points! You juked so many players! You looked really hot doing it! Say thank you. Give her a hug. And because it's dark in the bus, and the bus driver can't see you, don't let go. Your fellow classmates are singing the chorus of "Patience" by Guns N' Roses. Some are standing in the seats. Eve moves closer. Then, surprise: her mouth is on yours. Kiss her back. Don't mind that she tastes like garlic and kimchi—a pungency that will forevermore strike you as supremely erotic. Because right now, a new door is opening, and it's time to walk through it, together.

*

When it's time for your class to decide where to go for the senior class trip, don't vote for the option where you visit a third world country to help indigenous people build churches out of cinderblocks. Vote instead for the trip where you sail to the Bahamas, for *fun*. Waves? Beaches? Sun? It's a no-brainer. Especially when you remind yourself about the stories of previous senior class trips, and what other students have gotten away with. Imagine you might finally get some much-needed alone time with Eve. You can hope, at least. But not pray. This is not the kind of request you can bring to the Lord. Unless you include stuff like, *Keep me strong and pure*. Which you don't.

The bus ride to Miami takes an entire day. Wonder why—but don't question the fact that—boys and girls get to sit beside each other. Maybe it's because this is senior trip and you're big boys and girls. Maybe your sponsors are taking their own little vacation from their usual supervisory micromanagements. Whatever. Slump far enough in your seats so that the principal—who's driving the bus—can't see you in the rearview mirror. Spread a blanket over your laps. Slide your hands covertly—and for the very first time— into each other's jeans. Marvel at the warmth. The melty softness. "Oh my goodness," she whispers, "it's so *hard*." Hear footsteps. Retract hands. There, standing above you: your English teacher, on her way to the bathroom. "You guys *can't* be cold!" she exclaims, eyeing your blanket. Assure her that you are. Exchange knowing glances after she passes. Relish the resultant adrenaline blast. Acknowledge that what you just did was pretty crazy, that maybe a line needs to be drawn. Latch pinkies. Promise to return from this trip with virginity intact. Consciences assuaged, continue your furtive groping. As your hands fulfill their exploratory missions, pretend like you're interested in the plains of Florida as they sweep by outside. Note the egrets unfolding wings and, rising from swampland, flapping their angular bodies away.

*

Climb aboard a boat captained by a sun-dried, bandanna-and-braids-wearing Willie Nelson lookalike, a man who delivers a warning: "The ocean's rough today, kiddos." It's true. Once you hit the open sea, the waves are spectacular, smacking the hull, breaking into spray. Eve avoids getting seasick by swallowing a Dramamine and passing out in the sun. Meanwhile, you feel the swells down in the boat's kitchen as you chomp into a snack cake, and then take your place with the others alongside the railing, waiting to puke into the sea. Storms loom. Change course; instead of sailing to Grand Bahama, drop anchor at Bimini, a smaller island. Settle in. You're gonna be here awhile.

Don't ask why, after nearly four years of being monitored as closely and often as possible—there are stories that the Industrial Arts teacher skulks about after dark, hoping to catch students who've managed to escape the dorms without setting off the alarms—you're allowed to wander a Caribbean island completely unsupervised. Just do it. Stroll the length of the main street. Peek into dark bars where reggae music blasts from blown-out jukebox speakers. Buy T-shirts emblazoned with puffy sailboats from dreadlocked street vendors. Women with colored string plaited between their fingers will reach for Eve's hair—what beautiful braids they could make! Eve bashfully shakes her head. At a counter of a dingy restaurant, eat French fries and ice cream. In a hotel courtyard, find a doe-eyed toddler wandering around parentless. Take turns picking him up, holding him, and kissing him on the lips, pretending that he is your own.

Discover a soft footpath winding through grassy dunes to an empty beach. Palms sway in the wind, their leaves applauding. Find a shelf of sea rock to sit under. Unroll a towel. Prepare a clean, dry place. The sand—not the fine sugar of travel brochures—is coarse and sticky, laced with ribbons of seaweed and crumbly driftwood.

Suck lips and tongue and ears and neck. Pause, every few minutes, to make sure nobody's watching. Return, with vigor, to your dry humping. When Eve asks if you want to come in, just for a second, don't ask if she's sure. Just nod. In your head, think, *Just for a second*. You'll pop in— and out. And then you'll know. That's all you really want at this point: to know. To see. Eve mashes her bathing suit to one side. Position yourself. Slide in. Think, *Whoa*. A second passes. Then two. And more. More seconds are on their way. Does this count? You don't know. There's a song in your head: *It doesn't count if nothing comes out*. Eve clutches your arm. "Did you hear something?" she says. Stop breathing. Imagine the helmeted policeman you saw earlier. Imagine your principal—the man who, before you were officially together, once sent you both a letter, to say that even though he was led to believe you both were not engaged in "a relationship," that he had seen you both engaged in hand-holding, resting one's arms upon another, etc., and that if you failed to comply with the school's hands-off policy, he would have no choice but to "take action." Eve jumps up, scraping her face on the rock, ripping open her cheek. Offer your T-shirt—a tank top emblazoned with the letters R and E and M. Mop up the blood; assure her that she won't be scarred for life but worry that maybe she will be. A bird flies away.

Lead Eve back to the boats, where the food and medicine kits are stored in cardboard boxes. Tell everyone it happened as she was retrieving a sand dollar. Watch Eve snap open her compact mirror. Watch her run a finger—the one that's specked with brown scars, from when she was accidently splashed by boiling water as a baby—over the scabs, as if reading a kind of alien Braille. Don't argue when she says that this is punishment, sent special delivery by God for what you've done.

*

Upon returning to campus: act normal. Eat breakfast in the café. Pretend to sing during chapel. After lunch meet Eve in the school library, which as usual is empty. Spread *USA Today* out on a table and check your horoscopes. Normally, when nobody's around, or when Mrs. Fox, the librarian, carries her little pot to the water fountain to retrieve water for her plants, you make out furiously for ten seconds. Today, though, Eve's not in the mood. She has a question:

Do you regret what you've done? Squint. Pretend to think hard. Remember your first postorgasm thought: *This must've been how our first parents felt, in Eden, after they ate the forbidden fruit.* Remind yourself about what you heard about cultures where all a couple has to do to be considered married is to pledge their mutual love. Wonder if God honors those unions. If so, might He honor yours? And really, who's to say what God approves? Sure, there's the Bible, and it says what it says, but God could veto any part of it that He wanted, right? Tell Eve that you don't regret anything; tell yourself that it's assurance she wants. Don't imagine her engulfed in guilt. Promise her that you don't regret anything. You know what you did was wrong. You know—or hope—you'll be forgiven. You know an angel in heaven recorded every moment, but that Jesus's blood will blot out the bad parts. All you have to do is ask.

When Eve gives you watercolor paintings she's done of her invisible friend, Eun-Jin, it's okay to be confused: Eun-Jin is Eve's Korean name and the subject of the portrait is a sad circus clown with a long, Confucius mustache. Wonder if she's losing it. Turns out she has a legit reason to freak out: her period's late. Remind her that everything's gonna be okay, that nothing came out inside her, remember? Avoid thinking, *But what if something did?* You could be a father. At *seventeen.* What the hell would you do? Get a job? You have zero skills and—aside from making out with Eve—few passions. When you took the *What Color Is Your Parachute?* quiz in English class, you got "bus driver." When your faculty sponsor made predictions about future occupations for each member of your senior class, he predicted you'd be an attorney for the Los Angeles Lakers. You don't even like the Lakers, and the only attorney you know is an Audi-driving guy with hair plugs. You hate to even entertain the thought, but if it's true, if there's a tiny baby growing inside Eve right now, should she, like, *get rid of it*? According to Eve, the answer is yes: alone in her room, she punches herself in the stomach. Hard. You know because when nobody's looking she shows you how she does it. Then she does it again. And again. You have to physically stop her, which isn't easy. She's strong.

*

On graduation weekend, pack up your shit: your guitar, your flannel shirts, your tank tops, your photos tacked to the corkboard above your desk, your secret porn stash you harvested from other boys' supposedly secret porn stashes. Wonder how you're going to live without Eve, who broke up with you five times in the past week, if only because she thought that might be a workaround for the looming pain of missing you. After graduation, try to kiss her in front of her parents. When she moves her head at the last minute, get a mouthful of hair.

Move back to the mountains of southwestern North Carolina, to your parents' new house, the one they built on property that borders national forest. Get a job cashiering at McDonald's, where, because they ran out of hats, you're the only male employee who wears a visor. Learn the names and preferences of regulars; punch their orders in as soon as they walk in the door. At home write letters to Eve. Reduce yourself to a quivering, incoherent wad of desire. Tell her how much you miss and love her. Turn up The Cure's

Disintegration. Cue it to "Pictures of You." Tell her you're dying. Feel like you are.

Pick up the phone when it rings. "It started," Eve says. What she means: "I'm not pregnant." Say: "Thank God." She already has. For a long time, she hadn't prayed, hadn't thought she was worthy. Kept hitting herself in the stomach. But nothing worked—until she got down on her knees and asked for forgiveness. And that in the end was what unleashed the flow.

*

On Friday nights, drive south, through the mountains. Blast Nirvana and Alice in Chains for two and a half hours. Merge into traffic on I-75, get off on the exit for Duluth. Enter Eve's neighborhood—winding streets of conservatively regal brick homes—and park the car outside Eve's house. Don't get out. Instead, honk the horn, per her instructions. She's inside, lying to her parents, telling them she's going with a girl named Christy to the movies. Wait for her to come out—she sprints down the brick stairs bisecting her lawn. Drive away. Master the art of making out while piloting a car. Visit nearby parks. Look for foliage—thick enough so that when you enter it, you disappear. Glow. Ache.

If you arrive at Duluth early enough, you can hang at Eve's house before her mom gets back from the dental lab where she works, before her father returns home from the shop where he repairs and sells high-end wristwatches. Observe her house: the pale beige walls, the wooden cross hanging above the television, the family photo where nobody's smiling. Say yes to fried rice and kimchi. If her grandmother shows up—the one, when she found the pictures of you and Eve from the Bahamas, faces smashed against each other, windblown hair lashing your faces, shredded them into little pieces—hide behind the living room couch while Eve distracts her. Then bolt for your car.

*

At the end of summer, move to a Seventh-day Adventist College in Massachusetts, forty-five minutes from Boston, where Eve's studying engineering at a school you couldn't get into. Spend your first semester of undergrad in a quaint town that has rock walls and birch trees and historical markers every quarter-mile. Note that it's not unlike living in a Robert Frost poem. Attend classes in an old white house, once home to a long-dead philanthropist and financier, a building whose bedrooms, chock-full of desks bearing amusingly nonvulgar graffiti, have been converted into classrooms. Hang out in the house's living room, now a lounge, which resembles a cozy nineteenth-century library, what with its fireplace and lantern-style light fixtures and engraved tables where lamps cast yellow circles onto stacks of old *New Yorkers* and back issues of the school's literary journal. Take a seminar—Intro to the Renaissance—in the dining room, which has a long wooden table and arched, vine-enshrouded windows that reach nearly to the ceiling, allowing for stunning views of autumn foliage. It's like everything you know about what it means to love literature and high-mindedness and has become manifest in a single building, which is also home to the offices of teachers who've been studying books for decades. Read Kant and

Kierkegaard and Kafka and Keats. Write stunningly poor but passionately energetic imitations of Sylvia Plath and Anne Sexton and Robert Lowell. Walk around with the phrase "season of mist and mellow fruitfulness" playing on a loop in your head.

Smoke your first cigarette. Drink your first drink—Southern Comfort and lemonade—followed by your first second and first third drink in a row. Grip the sleeve of a leather jacket worn by a guy whom you just met as you puke into a toilet. Befriend guys like this leather jacket guy, guys who like to laugh and write poetry and play guitar, who show you aquifers and lakes and orchards and a haunted forest where a trail leads, inexplicably, to a Maharishi temple surrounded by lush lawns. Eat psychedelic mushrooms at somebody's parents' cabin in Maine and watch a gravel road transform into a ribbon of miniature skulls. Convince yourself that you're a living character in the book of your life. Wake up to being alive. Understand consciousness as a miracle. Get high at the local reservoir. Imagine that you have entered paradise. Joke that the distant geezer in a purple jogging suit is God, paying Earth a visit.

Stop going to church. Tell yourself it's no big deal, you're just taking a break. And you deserve one: for the first time in your life, nobody's making you go. Nobody's telling you to hurry up. Nobody's standing at the back of a sanctuary, searching for the back of your head, placing a checkmark by your name. It's weird; at boarding school, you never once skipped church or vespers, not once. It wasn't just that you didn't want to get in trouble—you'd be roombound for the rest of the weekend, forced to watch kids hang out at the center of campus from your window. You didn't want to miss anything. Most notably? The perfumed body of the girl you loved, dressed in her Sabbath finest.

*

That first winter in Massachusetts is the worst in one hundred years, or so they say. All you know is that whenever you step outside, the mucous in your nose instantly freezes. On Friday nights, pick up the T at Alewife, ride into downtown Boston to meet Eve. Hang your heads out of windows high above the ground to escape Eve's overheated dorm room and to blow plumes of smoke from hand-rolled cigarettes into falling snow. Visit all-ages clubs and dance under cascades of lasers. Eat squares of steaming pizza while walking through a blizzard. Visit a laundromat, write messages in Korean with your fingers in the steam of window glass. Have sex, but not frequently or well, in Eve's dorm room. Don't bother with prophylactics—neither of you is willing to admit that it's okay to fornicate, much less *make plans* to; it's just something that kinda happens. Suspect that what Eve needs is a detached lover, lounging coolly in perpetual satisfaction, someone she could rub herself on but who'd never give in. Problem is: you're neither cool nor satisfied. You're needy and impatient and gluttonous. Eve often swats you. "I'm full," she says. "Don't touch me." Try to leave her alone. Fail.

*

On Valentine's Day weekend, bring Eve a four-pack of miniature wine bottles and a heart-shaped box of chocolate.

When she's lying on her bed studying calculus in a T-shirt and a pair of your boxer shorts, decide to draw on her legs. A mural. A temporary tattoo. A blue face with a snake tongue. A monstrous mouth on her kneecap. Swirls. Dancing Matisse-like figures. When she asks you, out of the blue, if you'd ever do it with two women, feign thoughtfulness. Clear your throat. Cap a blue marker. Uncap a green. Then tell her that unless she had the power to clone herself . . . no.

Watch Eve roll over, raise her behind into the air, and slide her panties to one side. Circle a mole on her ass cheek.

"Come on," Eve says, flexing her cheeks. "Every guy wants to, right?"

Say you're not every guy.

"What makes you so different?"

Tell her that you love her.

"What if I told you that I knew a girl who was interested? No. I'm serious."

Ask her who.

"This girl. Jane. She's really pretty. Blonde."

Say, for Eve's benefit, that you're not into blondes.

"You'd like this one, though. She's got big boobs."

Shrug.

"Guys like big ones."

Say, "Whatever." Return to the devil on Eve's calf. Add flames.

"We were just talking. She was telling me about her ex. He goes to MIT. Sounded like a real jerk. Anyway, we were just talking and drinking some beer and playing around. I don't even know how it happened. But we kissed."

Repress a shiver when Eve shuts her eyes, lips parted slightly.

Say, "Uh-huh."

"Then my hand was up her shirt." Laugh. Leap off the bed. Tell her that this is stupid. That you refuse to believe it."

"Does it make you hot? We were *making out*."

Inquire, after she blows into your ear, only to quickly retreat, as to what happened next.

"Nothing. That was it."

Say, "Oh."

"So? Do you want to?"

Lie.

"Imagine it. Two women on top of you. Do you want it?"

Gaze out the window, to see snow falling. Again. Shrug. Then nod.

"Are you sure? Because I can call her right now if you want me to."

"Sure."

"Are you really really sure? Because you can't back out once we start."

"Yes! Yes, okay? Call her!"

Eve glares, shoves you with her foot. "Asshole."

Her eyes gleam with *I-knew-it!* dominance. She beat you again. Imagine, for a second, that she might spit on you. Watch your vision grow blurry, while ink bleeds into sheets.

*

Don't end it now. And don't end it later. In fact, don't *ever* end it, because you can't imagine a world without Eve, and because you don't want to. Don't end it when Eve suggests that you're no fun because you're sick of going to clubs, because you won't just loosen up and dance, and you don't like watching Eve grind on other guys. Don't end it when she belittles you in front of your friends, who, after she's gone, say, "Dude, why do you put up with that bullshit?" What they don't get: nobody knows Eve like you do. Even when she's being a defiant bitch, or when she says hurtful shit to prove that you're too soft and that you need to learn how to stand up for yourself, you know that down deep she really loves you. It would be easy to prove. You have it in writing.

*

Reconnect, over the phone, with a kid from grade school, one who you remember having to sleep in vacant hospital beds because his mother—a nurse—worked nights. He's going to apply to the University of North Carolina, where he plans to major in biology. He wants you to apply, wants to room together, promises that it'll be awesome, you'll go to basketball games, school's one of the best public institutions in the nation, it's way cheaper than what you're paying to attend an Adventist institution. Admit it: it sounds intriguing. You could graduate from a school nobody outside of the Adventist church had ever heard of, taught by teachers who, as good as they were, hadn't published much, if anything, outside of left-leaning Adventist publications, or you could transfer to a university that was world-renown, seeking instruction from teachers who'd published actual books with real presses, and whose stories had been featured in top literary magazines and, at least in the case of a teacher who'd written a story titled "Bobby Rex's Greatest Hit," turned into a TV movie.

Tell Eve a revised version of this story. Begin it by saying, "Hey, guess who called the other day trying to get me to transfer to UNC?" Deliver it in a kind of mocking way, and then say, "I told him it was a great idea, but I'd never leave Massachusetts." When Eve asks why, tell her that what you meant was: you'd never leave *her*. She laughs in your face. Act like you don't understand what's funny. Listen when she gives you a speech about how stupid it would be not to take this opportunity, and that you have to promise her that you'll make all future decisions without using her as a road block on your journey to being what you actually want to be, and what you know, in your heart, you already are: a writer.

*

Relocate to Carrboro, just outside of Chapel Hill, in an apartment that seems—at first—to be fine. So its color scheme is dingy. Beige walls, carpet. So the only overhead lights are in the kitchen and bathrooms. That's before your roommate starts decorating. Granted, it's only his room, but even having to glance inside—it doesn't exactly help the vibe. Dude cut out magazine photos of AIDS-ravaged patients and starving Ethiopian babies and dead bodies shot execution style in the ditches of remote countries and taped them to his walls, as if by surrounding himself with images of the destitute and terrorized, he might never forget how good he had it or how shitty others did, and thus spirits—if that's what you can say he had—would be lifted. Also on his wall: a strip of paper on which he'd written the number of days he estimated were remaining in his life. Don't bother trying to remember any of those numbers—it's a different sequence every time you look because he changes them daily—only that it's long enough to resist comprehension.

Go to the library. Search *New Yorker* archives for old, uncollected J. D. Salinger stories. Smoke weed. Listen to space rock and alt country. Try to keep up with the reading in Milton and Romantic Lit. Live off of cereal and stuff that's microwavable. Presume that, aside from your Shakespeare prof—a ruinous old jackass who claims that all you and your classmates care about is Mickey Mouse and Superman, and who gives you brutal fill-in-the-blank quizzes for each play—all your teachers are geniuses. Learn about the anthropological process of "strange-making" in your Southern Lit class, attend an African American funeral that becomes an occasion for the pastor to engage in a rousing rap-song-sermon calling out all the nonchurchgoing folk—*that means you*—to return to the fold. Listen to your philosophy professor—an Israeli woman—speculate about whether or not human beings can survive their deaths. Take notes while a grubby, white-haired, wildly bearded, sagelike Taoism prof illuminates, but not without a touch of sarcasm, the inherent paradoxes of the lives of sixth-century Taoist monks.

And when you're not marveling, wallow in misery.

Your main problem, aside from the fact that you miss Eve—a problem that is compounded, probably, by the fact that you smoke way too much weed—is that you have very few friends: your roommate, a few people you meet in creative writing workshops, primarily a guy with a pompadour who writes every one of his stories on a typewriter he found in a dumpster, and another kid who smokes unfiltered Pall Malls, drinks straight Jack Daniels, and gets pissed when everyone says that his stories remind them of Faulkner, even though Faulkner is his, like, personal hero.

Smoke pot. Like, a lot. Smoke at night to go to sleep. Smoke before you write. Smoke before class, sometimes, before you don your Rage Against the Machine T-shirt and your flared jeans and your Converse All-Stars and walk to class blasting the Beastie Boys *Ill Communication* on your Walkman. Tell yourself there's nothing wrong with getting high. You think better. You're more creative. When you're high, you feel connected to the universe. But you miss Eve. A lot. Call her. Leave messages. Wonder what she's doing, why she's not calling you back. Spend hours in the computer lab of the English Department, writing her long emails cataloguing your various miseries. Return to the apartment. Check your messages. It's Eve, she's calling to say she can't talk, she's going out, to a club, to a movie. She loves Boston so much! She can't imagine ever leaving.

*

If you possessed even the tiniest bit of foreknowledge, you'd be able to predict how this is going to end. Eve knows, because she's smart and because she thinks about shit way more than you. She'll blame herself for transforming you from happy, improvisational teenage comedian into sullen and clingy pothead. She'll know when it's time to take one for the team. She'll know it's for the best. She wouldn't be able to live with herself if she knew she would forever be the source of your sorrow.

Which is why she'll do what she does: call you up to tell you that she fucked somebody else. Listen, here, to your own voice, when you say stuff like, "It's okay" and "I understand" and "You made a mistake" and "We can work through this." You've lost your sense of who you are, your identity is too tied up with being her boyfriend, which is not who you used to be, back when you were oh-so-confidently wooing her, back when you were the popular kid who played guitar and got up in front of chapel during a talent show because somebody said, "Hey, Vollmer should do some impersonations," and everyone got on that bandwagon and so you stood up and made fun of all the faculty in front of the whole goddamn school. And everybody ate that shit up.

*

Now? Feel ashamed. Stupid. And—after walking downtown and downing three Long Island Iced Teas in a row—liberated.

*

After the breakup? Keep in touch. Transform yourself from "boyfriend" to "ex" to "friend she can now confide in about things that you would rather not know": that you weren't good at sex, that she had stopped being physically attracted to you, that the last guy she slept with had a dick the size of an extra-large banana.

Hear, as time passes, about her boyfriends. About dark nights. About blackouts. About passing out drunk in a snowdrift, only to be rescued by a tall, blond Swede who led her back to her room and tucked her into her bed and disappeared forever. "An angel," Eve insisted. "God still loves you."

Say, "So do I."

Keep saying this, for much longer than you need to—and longer than she does.

Fall, eventually, out of touch.

Try to write stories. Try to write *this* story. Fail, every time.

Go to grad school. Meet the hot, super-smart, blonde woman in your Shakespeare class who laughs uncontrollably at the same stuff as you—the word *bunghole,* for instance. Fall in love. Get married. Follow her to the Midwest, where she enters a PhD program and you fail to teach kids who grew up surrounded by cornfields how to make logical appeals. Procreate, without meaning to. Change diapers. Carry a toddler around in a backpack when you go to the grocery store. Argue about whether paint chips in your bathroom contain lead. Fight and make up. Keep working. Land jobs at a university in the southern Appalachians. Buy a house. Live, more or less, the exact life you once fantasized about as a kid growing up in the woods, wishing you lived with a woman you loved in a real town. A real neighborhood.

Think about Eve, from time to time. See her, occasionally, in your dreams, where the sight of her always fills you with a kind of giddy, teenage euphoria. Even after you think, *Oh shit, I'm already married*, you can't help but embrace her. Wake up hugging a pillow.

One day, when cleaning out a closet, find one of Eve's letters. Frown, because you thought you'd gotten rid of them all. This one's date bears the year of your college graduation, the summer you ran away to Wyoming to work at a national park, bussed tables at an inn whose lobby resembled something the Swiss Family Robinson would make out of varnished lodgepole pine. The letter's not long, one page, bears her signature scrawl, and doesn't say much except to note that *it's been one whole year since I did what I did* and *I remember that day* and *I know I hurt you* and *I lost a part of me* and *I look back and think how crazy things were* and *I'm not haunted* and *I have to be proud that I made the best of such a bad situation* and *I thought I should tell you, you're one of the best* and *you promised to be my friend* and *I hope things are better.* And then it ends the only way it could: *Love, Eve.*

Fold up the letter. Return it to the envelope. Slide the envelope into the first book you pull from the shelf, the Bible your parents gave you on your eleventh birthday, the day you were baptized, the one whose cover is emblazoned at the bottom with your full name in gold. Open your laptop. Log on to a popular social media website. Type Eve's name in the search box. Scroll down. Note that she likes Mighty Mighty Bosstones and Mitt Romney and follows *Fox News* and something called "Tea Party Patriots." Note how unsurprising this is; she did tend to insist, no matter what, that she was always right. Click on Photos. Check out the pumpkins she carved with her kids. The tunnels they dug through snow. The house they made out of gingerbread and colored frosting. Note that her husband—ghost white, with a ginger goatee—bears a strong resemblance to a famous comedian. Click New Message. Start typing: *Hey, it's been a long time.* Pause. Delete the sentence. Start typing again: *Dear Eve, This is going to sound weird, maybe, but I just wanted.* Delete. Repeat this process enough times to figure out that you won't be sending anything. Realize it's not a letter you need to write. You're done writing to Eve. Isn't that part of the reason why, last fall, you finally took the box of her letters you'd been carrying around your whole life and set them aflame, in the backyard of your new house, in what you assumed was a firepit? Six months later, you looked out the back window to see green stems had shot up from those ashes, and at their tips, little buds blooming bright yellow. This, you realize now, is nice to think about: a flower bed where a fire once burned. It's an image you could end with, if you ever decided you wanted to write this story, if you told yourself to just fucking do it, work backwards if you have to, then rearrange it all so that the starting point is where it ends: those blazing flowers, rising from a bed of the ashes of words you'll never read again.

KEEPER OF THE FLAME

On Thanksgiving my father and I went to visit the Nazi. That's what my father—a dentist to whom the Nazi had entrusted the care of his teeth—called him. As in: "Did I tell you who came into the office this week? The Nazi." And: "Did I tell you that I talked to the Nazi?" And: "You'll never guess what the Nazi told me." And so on.

We drove out of town on a narrow two-lane mountain road that wound past ramshackle houses and trailers using sheets for window curtains, over narrow bridges spanning rushing streams. We turned onto a gravel road, passed multiple signs announcing that we were now on private property and that potential trespassers would be shot. Eventually, we reached a softball-grade fence. My father dialed the Nazi's number on his phone and the front gate glided backwards on lubed wheels. We drove inside and the house, which resembled a castle, came into view. It wasn't exactly *Neuschwanstein,* but it had rock walls and turrets and wooden doors with wrought iron hinges and arched windows. It had a fountain and an impressive series of stairs leading to the front door. The whole thing looked like something a government—though certainly not our own—had erected centuries before.

The Nazi's garage door—like the front gate—opened automatically, by some unseen force, and after it slowly retracted itself, my father and I entered. Seconds later, another door opened, and the man himself—the Nazi—appeared. Tall and hearty, with a head of dirty blond locks cut in a quasi bowl cut, his long bangs flapped when he walked. His wife looked like she might've been created in a laboratory funded by the Third Reich: her hair—so blonde it was nearly white—fell in a luminous sheet down her back. She was tall and wide-eyed, her lips crimson. She introduced and immediately excused herself, and our tour began.

The interior of the Nazi's home was immaculate and clutter-free. There were no stacks of bills or mail on the counter, no dish of change, no stray pens, no stacks of coasters, no knickknacks on the windowsills, no stained glass butterflies affixed to the windowpane above the kitchen sink. No family photographs—no photographs of any kind—hung from the walls. Papers and pictures and notes and calendars had not been affixed via magnets to the fridge, whose door remained utterly blank. Empty tabletops—devoid even of napkin holders or salt and pepper shakers—gleamed. The place felt sanitized, sterile. Here, at the home of the Nazi, a person seemed unlikely to catch any sort of disease. Rooms had been reduced to the bare minimum. Stuff—if stuff existed here—lived behind closed doors.

The Nazi led us up a flight of stairs, to a balcony overlooking the living room. He then opened an impressive wooden door—all the doors in the house were arched and hinged with wrought iron—to reveal yet another door, this one constructed from what appeared to be bomb-shelter-grade metal, and upon whose surface the words "Danger: High Voltage" had been emblazoned. The Nazi unlocked and then swung open this hatch-like door, and we descended a steep spiral staircase, passing near the top a recessed statue: a sculpted head of a soldier wearing an SS helmet. Down, down, down we went, around and around we wound, so far in fact I could feel a change in temperature. Once we'd reached the bottom, the Nazi swung open an iron gate and flipped a switch.

The resultant clack reverberated. Light flooded the room, revealing a cathedral-like space with thirty-foot-high ceilings and a marble floor bearing the image of a sun wheel. At one end of the room hung a massive tapestry bearing the image of the Tree of Life, which had, the Nazi claimed, as a pre-Christian pagan symbol, been important to the founding members of the Third Reich. Beneath this, a pulpit-like table displayed two wooden boxes, each bearing lightning-shaped Ss. These boxes, the Nazi had explained, had been made especially to hold copies of *Mein Kampf* and served as gifts for SS officers on their wedding days: a token of the Führer's appreciation.

Elsewhere: glass shelves of Hitler Youth daggers, polished and dangerously sharp; an SS officer's ring, into which had been carved a grinning Totenkopf; ceramic platters embossed with Runic symbols; a hand-carved wooden plate depicting the Wewelsburg Castle, where Himmler hoped to reconvene the Arthurian Knights of the Round Table; a chair from the same castle's great hall, leather

bolted to its back and seat; a set of silver, whose handles had
been engraved with Sig runes, and which had purportedly
come from the Eagle's Nest—the alpine chalet presented to
Hitler on the occasion of his fiftieth birthday.

My father glanced over his shoulder at me and emitted
a wheeze-burst of laughter—an exhalation intended to
express disbelief. He had led me to an underground vault
containing the artifacts of the past century's most brutal
regime, and he now seemed downright giddy. I, on the
other hand, found it difficult to process what any of this
meant. That is, I didn't know why it was here, how it had
gotten from where it had been made, and where it was
now. Were we in the presence of some kind of monster? Or
had he created this space for stuff he deemed historically
significant, buried it in a moisture-controlled vault because
he fancied himself one of history's unbiased curators? Was
this the product of an obsessive and sympathetic mind, one
that interpreted the mainstream records of history as having
been unduly cruel to the Third Reich, which had been a
movement, in his eyes, about nationalism, about ancestors,
about revering and honoring the past? I didn't know. And I
was afraid to ask.

*

The Nazi handed me a black German helmet and explained
why it was rare: all helmets of this particular kind, once the
war started, had been recalled and painted in field colors.
To find one that remained unaltered was exceedingly
uncommon. And "exceedingly uncommon" translated into

"quite valuable." The helmet, if the Nazi saw fit to sell it, might fetch upwards of thirty thousand dollars.

Normally, my father explained, as if to better help me appreciate the objects before me, collectors of Third Reich militaria collected one—or mostly one—kind of artifact, attempting to amass an anthology of one specific relic. The Nazi nodded. Some collected knives, some helmets, some field jackets, some medals. The difference in this collection was that it wasn't a collection of only one thing. It was a collection of many things. The scope of this collection was greater. And therefore, it was more singular.

For example, there were the mannequins.

There were four mannequins, actually, each dressed in a different uniform. This uniform included field jackets, pants, belts, medals, shoes, knives, and belts. Apparently, the Nazi had purchased these mannequins from various department stores and carted them back to his castle, where he sawed off the heads. He then fashioned new heads—the Nazi, in another life, had worked in advertising and was something of an artist—and then—as if they were his own personal life-sized dolls—he'd dressed them in SS uniforms.

The mannequins represented, as far as was possible, a reconstruction of a particular soldier. That is, the Nazi had found a uniform and tracked down as many records of the actual soldier to whom it'd belonged. He'd identified and tracked down other possessions that belonged to the solider. He knew the soldier's rank, his shoe size, his hair and eye color, knew exactly how many medals that particular soldier had received. The Nazi could tell you what this soldier's favorite food had been, whether he'd been sick or injured or killed, and whether he'd suffered disciplinary action.

I would like to say that I was disgusted, that the sight of the Nazi clothing and gear stirred some powerful revulsion, but down there, underground, I felt the seductive pull of visual design. The clarity and symmetry, the contrast of the red and white and black, the crisp lines and borders, the mysterious symbols, the glossy belts, the gleam of polished buckles— these uniforms, tools, weapons, helmets, and flags had been assembled by intelligent artists from the finest and heartiest earthly materials. I hate to admit that these things were beautiful but I had no other choice. To *not* say they were beautiful would be to diminish their power. And their power—however awful—demanded to be recognized.

*

"This," my father said, "is history."

That is, he might've said, "This is history." I don't know. My memory can't be trusted. I know I was there at the Nazi's house; I know that I wandered a cathedral-like space and looked dead mannequins in the eye and feared that they would, if I continued to stare, awaken. But I can't remember everything—or, honestly, much of anything— that was said. What strikes me more was the mood of my father (gleeful, reverent, inquisitive) and the mood of the Nazi (not cheerless and not cheerful but, rather, despite being focused, detached). I do know that my father said, as the Nazi retrieved for us some glittering knife or piece of china, that "it always makes me nervous" when he, the Nazi, took something out of the case—meaning that he worried that one of these artifacts might be harmed. But the Nazi did not approach these objects with reverence. He didn't need to. The space in which they existed had already offered them as objects to be revered.

*

Before we left the Nazi's sanctuary slash museum slash dungeon and ascended to the kitchen, where the Nazi's wife poured us coffee and offered us a platter of cookies; before the Nazi took a cookie, saying they never kept this kind of stuff—meaning sweets—in the house; before the Nazi's wife reminded us that there had also been concentration camps in America, that it had been a time of war, that of course the camps had been such terribly awful places, but awful things had gone on in so many places the world over; before any of that happened—the Nazi wanted to show us one last thing. This last thing was kept inside a glass case with a glass lid, which the Nazi opened. He secured the lid so that it wouldn't fall, then opened an old leather-bound book and began flipping through its yellow pages. It was a ledger of sorts and inside it were the names of hundreds of SS officers. Finally, he pointed to a column of names. The surname was the same as the one that belonged to my father and me. The Nazi didn't say, "Looks like your Uncle Walt was an SS man." He didn't say, "See, you do have Nazis in your family." He just tapped the name with his finger. It was as if he wanted this—the fact that people with the same surname as ours had served under Hitler—to sink in on its own. To show us that whatever we might think about the Nazis, we were in fact connected, by the very name that I'd thought, as a child, separated our family from everybody else's.

*

The sun had fallen below the ridgelines by the time we left the Nazi's castle. My father drove us home. He wondered aloud what would happen to the Nazi's stuff when the man met his demise, wondered if the Nazi had insured all those relics, and where his last will and testament—supposing he'd drawn one up—stipulated they would go. My father seemed concerned about the Nazi and his legacy, partly because he admired the lengths that the Nazi had gone to in order to amass such a collection, and partly because he seemed to think of the man as a friend. "A friend?" I said. I was incredulous. I said no way could he be friends with a man he merely humored, that true friends weren't afraid to say what they thought, which was that the Nazi was (at best) misguided and (at worst) a lunatic; that he had constructed, unbeknownst to all the people living in trailers and cabins along this road, a private shrine to the Third Reich; that he apparently thought Heinrich Himmler was a character worthy of admiration; that he obviously thought the Holocaust hadn't existed—at least not in the way most understood it; and that unless my father had come out and said what he truly believed, he was silently endorsing the Nazi's viewpoints. I can't remember how or even if my father had defended himself against these accusations, but I know he didn't say what I'm thinking now—that I had no room to talk. I'd said very little—if anything—during our visit. Though my mind had been lurching most of the time, seeking any sort of anti-Nazi argument, I'd feared that nothing I could drum up would be able to contend with the Nazi's own encyclopedic knowledge. I'd even begun to wonder how I'd come to know what I knew, and how it was that I could prove beyond a shadow of a doubt that the Nazis were guilty of the crimes with which they'd been accused. In short, I had done nothing and said nothing to give the Nazi one single reason to think I wasn't on his side. For all he knew, I might've been a man on a pilgrimage, coming to pay homage to the ephemera of a lost and once-glorious empire. After all, he had pointed to my name in a directory listing the names of former Nazis—and I hadn't protested. I had thought, *Wow, that's messed up*. But I hadn't said a word.

NEVER FORGET

No one now living knows much about the massacre at Draper's Meadow. No witness to the events ever penned an account, and most—if not all—renderings of the events can be traced to a couple of reports written by descendants of the victims. We don't know the exact location of the massacre, though it's safe to say that it took place somewhere on the campus of Virginia Tech, most likely in the vicinity of the Duck Pond, a place Blacksburg residents now visit to seek solace: to fish for mud bass, to feed mallards and Muscovy and Canadian geese, to stroll paths creased with frost heaves, to stare at rippling water. Nor do we know what motivated the band of Shawnee Indians to attack this place, once home to a group of enterprising trans-Allegheny pioneers. The explanation given by John Ingles, a descendant of one of the survivors, who claimed that the Shawnee simply had "a heathen thirst for bloodshed and plunder," smacks of the kind of racism that justified the denigration—and thus persecution—of an entire country's worth of indigenous people. And while the Shawnee had plenty of reasons for attacking a white settlement—after all, these farmers had claimed land that, by some accounts, had once been sacred hunting ground—it's also possible that the Indians had targeted Draper's Meadow because the French, as part of their new alliance against the British at the outset of the French and Indian Wars, had promised compensation for the scalps of Englishmen. This premise is especially alluring when one considers that the victims of the attack included Colonel James Patton, a formidable—if somewhat arrogant and opportunistic—Irish sea captain and frontiersman, who, in his dealings with Indians and whites alike, had made a good many enemies, and who—it is presumed— had broken away from a supply train to pause at Draper's Meadow, possibly for recuperative purposes.

We don't know which settler spotted the Indians first. We're told that Mrs. George Draper, who yelled the first warning, afterward ran into her cabin to retrieve her baby, only to be shot in the arm as she fled, causing her to drop her infant child, whom the Shawnee scooped up and whose head they dashed against the ends of cabin logs. Should we believe that Colonel Patton, described by others as "robust" and "Herculean," was sitting at a writing desk in his primitive dwelling when he heard Mrs. Draper's warning cry? That he grabbed his broadsword and strode out the cabin's front door, where, before being shot dead, he struck down two of his attackers? We don't know how the Indians slew their remaining victims, or whether they scalped them. We know only that some died, while others—perhaps those who appeared to be in better shape and could therefore help replenish the recently diminished Shawnee population— were taken captive, one of whom happened to be Mary Draper Ingles, whose story of escaping the tribe once they reached Ohio and returning to Virginia on foot and possibly unclothed, alongside an old Dutch woman who may or may not have tried to eat her—*twice*—is a tale often told in these mountains. We know the Indians set fire to the buildings, but not how, whether they arrived bearing torches or used fireplace logs already burning. We're told that the Indians' last act, subsequent to setting the settlement ablaze, was to decapitate a man named Philip Barger, and to deliver a sack containing his head to Mrs. Philip Lybrook, who lived in a cabin with her husband at the mouth of Sinking Creek. Did the Shawnee speak English, and did they, as legend has it, instruct Mrs. Lybrook to look inside the bag, in order to "find someone she knew"? How much time passed before Draper's and Ingles' husbands, who escaped capture or death by working in the nearby wheat fields, looked up from their work and saw smoke rising above the trees? No one can say. We don't know if any of the victims were still alive once these men reached the settlement, or if these farmers braved flumes of heat to drag the bodies away from the fire, or if instead they had to wait until the bodies— aswarm with green iridescent flies—had already cooled.

One of the few things we do know for sure is that no trace of these settlers' cabins remains. When I say *we*, it's not even clear what I mean. The massacre, which I've rarely, if ever, heard anyone talk about, has been largely forgotten. The majority of Blacksburg's current residents seem largely unaware of the event. It's true that a number of historical markers commemorate the event but these markers are hard to find. There's a tarnished metal plate, upon which has been engraved a dedication to those who lost their lives on that day, bolted to a rock embedded in the ground on a hillock not far from the President's House. A stone ledge, buried in the earth on the northeast side of the Duck Pond, bears the following words: DRAPER'S MEADOW MASSACRE, JULY 8, 1755. It's easy to imagine visitors reading this inscription and having no idea what to make of it, of bypassing "Draper's Meadow" and the date, and zeroing in on the word *massacre*, and that particular series of letters delivering them to an altogether different time and place.

*

Two hundred and fifty-two years after the Draper's Meadow massacre, on the 16th of April, the weather is lousy, and I— on my way to Virginia Tech, where I teach creative writing and freshman composition—am out in it: jogging through a blizzard of stinging flakes to a bus stop. Snow churns in the gusts, seems never to land, fails to accumulate. The bus arrives, its digital readout flashing BUS FULL. I curse, expecting it to pass, but it stops and the doors unfold and I board sheepishly, hope that—as I flash my university ID— the driver failed to read my lips. I hook my arm around a silver post; the bus—packed with sleepy undergraduates, the air sweet with the smell of shampoo and cologne— lurches forward. A sullen, chubby girl eats Cheerios from a plastic bag. Another girl, slowly chewing gum, types on her phone with her thumbs. I stare at the patchy beard of a droopy-lidded guy who suddenly yawns so intensely it appears he might be in danger of dislocating his jaw.

What I don't know, what nobody else on this bus knows: two people have been shot in a dormitory on the west side of campus. These people are now dying; perhaps they are already dead. Had someone announced this news to the bus, riders would've surely murmured or winced or lifted their eyebrows. Some would've exhaled curse words, drawn them out slowly, holy this or holy that, flipped open a phone to check the news. But the bus would've kept going. It wouldn't have turned around. Nobody would've gotten off at the next stop, because nobody ever gets off at the next stop—somebody always gets on. Those students who were headed to the building where, in less than half an hour, hundreds of bullets would be fired into the bodies of forty-seven people, would not re-chart their courses. They would continue onward. They would hope that the people who'd been shot would be okay and that the police would apprehend the shooter. They would remember the schizophrenic homeless dude from the beginning of the year, the one who'd shot an officer on the Huckleberry Trail, the ribbon of asphalt leading from downtown Blacksburg to the New River Valley Mall in Christiansburg. They would assume—as I surely would have—that by the time we reached campus, someone, somewhere, would have things under control.

*

The bus stops at McBryde Hall, one building from Norris, the site where Sueng Hui Cho will fire 170 rounds into the bodies of forty-seven students and faculty, and I disembark. I walk a hundred yards east, enter Shanks Hall, and climb four flights of stairs to my office, where I pour coffee from a thermos into a thermos cap and check my email and work on a story I've been writing about a dentist whose wife dies on his honeymoon, following an allergic reaction to a manta ray sting. I'm listening to a band called Deerhunter on iTunes as I read the last chapters of *American Pastoral,* a book by Philip Roth that concerns a guy named Swede, a former high school basketball star who takes over his father's glove factory and marries Miss New Jersey and produces a daughter who later becomes a domestic terrorist.

Wife who dies. Hunter. Domestic terrorist. I fail to note the thematic connection between these words, and thus the synchronicity fails to make itself known. A beep sounds; I click a postage stamp on my screen. The email, from University Relations, explains that a "shooting incident" has occurred and that everyone at Tech should contact the VT Police if they spot anything "suspicious." Word in the building is that it's a drug deal gone bad, and that the shooter's been identified as a student from nearby Radford University. *Whatever,* I think, and return—relatively unconcerned—to my reading. The book's amazing; I'm completely absorbed. Twenty-five minutes later, another email: "A gunman is loose on campus. Stay in buildings until further notice." *Whoa,* I think. *Crazy.* I shut my book, close my office door, call my wife, Kelly, who tells me to be careful. I check the *Roanoke Times* website and CNN and *Washington Post.* Nothing.

A megaphone system announces, "This is an emergency. Seek shelter immediately. Stay away from windows." I immediately disobey this command, wheeling my chair to my window, which looks out onto a dormitory and a slice of Turner Street, and the Burger King on the other side. A couple of ambulances speed past. I am not alarmed. I don't think, *Those are for the dead and dying.*

Three girls, wearing coats and pajama bottoms, emerge from the dorm next door. They light cigarettes. They yell something incomprehensible and defiant. They laugh.

They don't yet know.

Neither do I.

*

The first number I hear is one. Then three. Then twenty. *Twenty* students. *Killed.* Professors, grad students, and stunned undergraduates who had obeyed the commands of the public address system begin to emerge from offices, whispering huskily. Should we stay? Is it over? Finally, somebody says, "I don't know about ya'll, but I'm getting the hell outta here."

I follow a professor—a tall, thin man with hunched shoulders and horn-rimmed glasses—to the parking lot. Nobody told us we were free to leave, nobody knows if we need permission, nobody knows if it—whatever "it" is—is over. On the way to the parking lot, I feel exposed, permeable. I envision the sting of a sniper's rifle, the pop of gunfire. I eye every stranger we pass, and every distant figure, with suspicion. I tell myself to act normal—whatever that means. It's like one of those dreams I have where I find myself in a public place without clothes, or I've forgotten to wear pants, but I've convinced myself that I can survive the situation by acting like nothing is wrong. By the time we reach the parking lot, my pulse has quickened. Inside the car, I have to fight the urge to slump to the floor, or at least below the window. I glance into the rearview mirror, where the professor's eyes are wide, bulging as he slides his key into the ignition. His face is pale and expressionless. He says, "This is huge. This is big time. Everybody's going to know somebody."

In my head, I fill in the words he'd omitted: *who has died.*

*

At home, Kelly and I lock our doors and windows. We still don't know whether what's happened is over, and as absurd as it would seem for the shooter to end up inside our house, we aren't taking any chances. A tear in the fabric of everyday life has been opened, chaos has been unleashed, and we need to secure ourselves. Problem is, our family is incomplete: Elijah, our three-and-a- half-year-old son, is still in preschool. We debate whether we should walk past the cul-de-sac at the end of the street and then through a stand of pine trees and then across another street to the Church of the Brethren and retrieve him. We've heard that all schools in the county are on lockdown. We also know that, during the day, the doors of the church remain unlocked, and that—under normal circumstances—anybody can stroll right in, at any time. We tell ourselves that Elijah will be safe there, in rooms stacked to the ceiling with board games and Tupperware containers of toys, a place where the white-bearded Mr. Bungard and the white-haired Ms. Noni, with their extraordinary powers of persuasion, are able to convince a dozen three-year-olds to eat their snacks quietly, while sitting on a single blanket, all facing the same direction. We assume our fear is unwarranted, but still, we would like to bring him home, to lock and dead-bolt the doors and hold him, to know for sure that he's safe—despite the fact that he is not the kind of child who really—if ever—wants to be held, mainly because he refuses to sit still. In the end, we defer to the judgment of Ms. Noni, who tells us over the phone that there's no reason to interrupt him, that he's playing happily with his friends. And so, we postpone our retrieval and pray we're doing the right thing.

*

We watch TV with our laptops open, refreshing CNN and Fox and *The New York Times*. Our inboxes have been flooded with email. We field calls, try to return messages, but it's difficult; we keep losing signals. The wind's insane—too strong, we learn, for helicopters to airlift wounded. Lights blink. Clocks flash wrong times. The TV goes black, then bursts suddenly to life. Each time, the clamor startles us.

We flip channels, seeking eyewitness accounts. We want a justification, however absurd. We want to know how and why this happened, and who was responsible. But we also want names. We need to know if anyone we know was among those who were injured or slain.

As I picture the faces of my students, I am overcome by an unexpected and desperate fondness for each of them, regardless of how much grief they've given me: Jessica, the blonde Republican who'd campaigned the previous semester for a state senator; John, the meek speed-metal guitarist; Matt, the droopy-lidded stoner; Amanda, a girl who's obsessed with—much to my dismay—Duke basketball; Brendan, a kid who unironically loves Carnival Cruises; the girl with the last name Butt; the guy with the last name Christ.

Some respond to my emails. Most say they're okay; others aren't sure. Some know people who were shot, others are waiting to hear back. All are shocked and horrified, but thankful someone's asked how they are. I imagine entering a classroom and realize I have no idea what to do. Narrowing research questions, choosing genres, constructing thesis statements, arriving at conclusions: it all seems shamefully, preposterously irrelevant.

*

The final count is thirty-two—thirty-three, if you're feeling generous enough to count the shooter. Many aren't. And don't.

The victims include: a former coffeehouse singer, a master's student researching the sustainability of water quantity during drought, a triple major who played the baritone in the band, an effervescent French teacher, a skilled horsewoman, an accomplished swimmer, a triathlete who also happened to be a top researcher in biomechanics, a master's student researching stormwater management, a residence hall advisor who cared for her residents as if she were their mother, a teaching assistant who'd been credited with discovering the first West Nile virus–infected mosquito in Centre County, an accomplished classical pianist with dreams of studying nanotechnology, an award-winning engineering student, a member of the cadet jazz band, a PhD student in civil engineering, a world-renown hydrologist, and a Holocaust survivor.

The accompanying photos showcase the obliviousness of innocence. Studying them, reading the biographies, I can't help but wonder if Norris Hall had been an arbitrary choice on the part of the shooter, or whether he'd done his research, and targeted the building that held the highest percentage of the university's overachievers, and said to himself, *Yes,* this *will be my final destination.*

*

At the entrances to our buildings, signs appear—not paper signs but plastic ones, their surfaces seared with maroon letters that read: "Media, please respect our mourning." This is, for the media, an impossible request to honor. Mourning is a main staple of the media's diet, and therefore what it continuously hunts. The media, when it asks how we're doing, hopes our answer is: "Not well." The media snakes its tentacles into the cracks of a tragedy, feeling, probing, asking: *What can I find? Is it sharp enough? Dangerous enough? Sad enough?* If the answer is yes, then it slaps on its suckers, nabs it, shows it to anyone who will watch, moves to the next thing.

And let me be clear: I'm one of those watchers. In fact, I seem to be defined at this moment only by my insatiable need to consume news coverage. For hours, I flip between channels, worried that I'm on the wrong one, that the one I'm not watching is the one broadcasting the information I need. I learn that Professor Libriscu barricaded the door with his body so students could line up at the windows and leap out; that Kevin Granata tried to tackle the gunman; that a girl who'd been shot twice in the head had survived by playing dead, hiding her phone in her hair as she whispered to 911 dispatch; that the cell phones of dead students were ringing as responders lugged body bags from the building. I am absorbing more information than I know what to do with. My head feels like it's housing a snowstorm of static. My eyes burn. I flit between channels and browser windows. I don't know what I'm looking for. It is too early to accept the truth: that there is no information that will explain what has happened, and that such an explanation will never arrive.

Meanwhile, the campus has become a prop, a setting, a backdrop for a particular kind of event: the media-glutted aftermath. "Here we are at Virginia Tech," the reporters say, "the scene of the largest mass murder in American history." The largest. The worst. The deadliest. The tragedy is, they insist, something that can—and must—be measured. They might as well be saying: *Here we are at the worst thing of all time.*

The *V* and *T* accompanying the headlines begin to assume foreboding qualities—like the blunt ends of these letters might be used to bludgeon someone. Cable news stations have created special logos for this story. The *Virginia Tech* in the "Virginia Tech Massacre" starts to look like the logo of a corporate sponsor, like the massacre had been an event subsidized by the school.

A reporter tells a student—one who appears on several different channels in the same gray Virginia Tech sweatshirt—that some are calling him a hero. What does the student think of that? The student tries to speak but can't. His face contracts; he's trying to stop himself from crying. Unlike the reporters, he's exhibiting restraint.

He quenches a couple of sobs, squeaks out: "I'm just glad to be here." *Glad to be here,* I think. He's glad to be alive. It's the only thing he knows for sure.

The anchorman of *Headline News* says, "Mm." He jerks once in his chair, the way a dead body might were it to receive a sudden surge of electricity. "Raw emotion," he says, as if naming something foreign, a phenomenon he's read about and can therefore only try to imagine.

*

Two days after the shootings, Kelly and I attend the convocation, which is held in Cassel Coliseum, the university's basketball arena. By the time we arrive, the coliseum's full, so we—with the rest of the overflow crowd—are directed to neighboring Lane Stadium, where we sit under a blazing sun, a sky now blue. Every fall, fans congregate here to eat monolithic turkey legs and cheer the Hokie defense as it incapacitates opponents. Now, the face of the President of the United States appears on the screen of the Jumbotron. It is the head of a man who, four years before, supported the preemptive invasion of a country that posed a theoretical threat to our national security. Depending on which statistical records you believe, this invasion may have killed and wounded as many as hundreds of thousands of innocent people. The head, which attempts to look serious, says that it is filled with sorrow, and that someday, whether we can picture it now or not, things will return to normal.

Members of the Virginia Tech administration take turns saying things they think we want to hear, things that—I presume—they want to hear themselves say. One of our poets—our most famous—stands to speak. She wears a black suit, a white shirt, a loose black tie. She begins with an assessment—"We are sad today"—and ends with a prophecy: "We will prevail." I don't know what to think about this. Of course I want to think that we will prevail—whatever that means. Still, I can't help but think, *Already*? Are we *already* thinking about prevailing? Didn't the shootings happen only two days ago? Weren't they *still* happening, in some sense? Weren't they stuck on repeat in our heads? Weren't we reliving them in our dreams?

The Jumbotron's malfunctioning. Its words: indecipherable. Everything sounds like it's underwater, like it's been reverbed and delayed. The sun—a brutal light—bears down on us. We exit the stadium thirsty and sunburned. On the way out, I pick up a *Collegiate Times* newspaper. On the back page, Lockheed Martin—the largest manufacturer of weaponry in the world—has printed its condolences.

In other news, auditions for *Girls Gone Wild* have been canceled.

*

At our departmental meeting, the room is packed: TAs, professors, faculty I've never seen before. I wonder who had the shooter in class, who knew him, who feels responsible. I wonder who refuses to feel responsible, since what could he or she have really done when faced with a person who'd nurtured such monstrous desires?

I keep these inquiries to myself.

Refreshments—seven-layer dip, Fritos, pound cake—have been arranged on a folding table. Representatives from Human Resources take turns at a podium: a tall guy with a radio voice, a man who looks like he could play a doctor on TV, a woman who apologizes for being soft-spoken. We collect handouts that include the phrase *grief management*. A woman said to be an authority in these matters informs us that we should engage in something creative. We might find it comforting, she says, to do something with our hands. We might, she supposes, find solace in gardening. I clench my jaw. I shake my head. It is not the idea of finding solace that angers me. It's that the institution where I work would presume to tell me—or anyone else—where we might find it.

*

After the meeting, Kelly and I decide to take a walk through campus. We exit Shanks—the building that houses our department—and for the first time, the sight of the building's name on the sign outside suggests homemade weaponry. I do not mention this to Kelly. I don't say anything. Neither does she.

We pass Norris, the building where the shootings took place. I wonder what it looks like in there, whether there are people, as police tape thrashes in the wind outside, scrubbing bloodstains. Reporters wander the Drill Field, interviewing students, who themselves are wandering. Classes have been canceled. People—people whom the students knew, whom they didn't know, whom they knew of, whom they now know of, whom they remembered and don't—have been shot and killed, in a building they pass everyday, in classrooms where they've doodled and snoozed, jotted notes and drawn graffiti. They don't know what to do or where to go, and wherever they go seems like the wrong place to be. They flock to Kentucky Fried Chicken. They nap on the floor of the local Blockbuster. They place stuffed animals wearing little T-shirts with VT logos upon makeshift shrines. They stand blinking and cold before great waxen candleblobs that rarely flicker with light; the wind keeps blowing them out. They hold signs that say, "Free Hugs and Hershey Kisses." They enter great blue-and-white-striped tents tethered to the Drill Field, where long, white, wooden boards—literally dozens of them—bear thousands of messages:

"NeVer ForgeT."

"I never knew any of you. I will miss you all."

"There are 32 angels in heaven today explaining what a HOKIE is."

"32 gone. Because 1 was lost."

"Dear Cho, Sleep in peace and let all the things that hurt you a lot go."

"I'm sorry I couldn't do more."

I too feel compelled to write something, to put my name on one of these gigantic sympathy cards that will be later archived in University Storage. The problem is that I have no idea what to write. I'm crippled by self-consciousness and the notion that anything I could possibly write would be interpreted as laughably inadequate. It seems futile to address the dead. It seems brash to make pronouncements. And it seems presumptuous to make public my own private and conflicted sentiments. Also, there's the additional problem of not knowing exactly what I *do* feel. Even if I did know, what good would it do me—or anyone else? And why would my *feelings*—of all things—matter? The only thing that matters, it seems, is that the sons and daughters of mothers and fathers are now gone forever. And no amount of never forgetting will ever bring them back.

*

Our wandering brings us to the Inn at Virginia Tech, where skirted banquet tables offer faux-silver platters of granola bars and snack cakes, bowls of apples and oranges and bananas—nourishment for the grieving, for those who are investigating the source of the grief, and for those reporting it. A wall-sized screen in a conference room plays news footage, which, when we pass it, features a still photo of the shooter. His head, which fills the screen, is at least half a story tall. It has spoken more since it perished than it did during the past twenty-two years.

The psychotic nature of the shooter's photos seems manufactured. Maybe, I think, he *wanted* to be crazy. Then again: what do I know about mental health? About psychology? About anything? There are no answers—only facts. The shooter wrote stories and plays and poems about sexual abuse and violence. He had an imaginary girlfriend named "Jelly." He refused to speak. He said that he didn't have a choice: he had to kill. He said someone could've stopped him. He wanted to be referred to as a question mark.

In another conference room, two hundred people are being debriefed. Earlier, a woman—a psychologist—had explained how to stop yourself from crying during television interviews: move your fingers and toes. This physical activity will trick your brain and stop your tears. Now, someone's reading names from the list of the injured, none of which I recognize. Are the people in this room family members of the victims? If so, I feel bad that we've intruded. But I don't know what else to do. I feel terrible if I take my mind off the shooter and victims. I feel terrible if I keep my mind on the shooter and the victims. Feeling terrible, it seems, is my new vocation, one that—despite how easy it seems—I feel like I'm failing.

I feel disconnected and empty and ashamed for wanting to feel something other than what I do, part of which is: *I could've been there.* If I'd been there, if I'd borne witness to the barrage of bullets, I'd have earned the right to wonder why I'd survived, why I—and not others—had been spared. To not be dead and not be a survivor—and to not personally know anyone who had died—was to not know one's place in the tragedy. You were there but you weren't. You'd forever be associated with a disaster you hadn't experienced, a storm whose epicenter remained hidden. You'd feel sad but not sad enough. You'd want to grieve but couldn't—and it'd feel false if you had.

*

On the way back from the inn, an adolescent girl with dark curly hair stops us. She introduces herself and her brother, a younger redhead with freckles. "I just wanted to let you know that God loves you," she says. "Do you know that?" Though I am a believer, I am dissatisfied and opposed to overly sentimental portraits of the divine. But this girl's bold proselytizing catches me off guard. I tell her that yes, we do know that God loves us.

"Do you know for a fact that if you died today you would go to heaven?"

Despite the fact that this subject is more complicated—from my perspective—than a yes or no, I realize we've been caught, and I say, "Uh, yeah."

The girl continues. "On a scale of 1 to 10," she says, "how would you measure how on fire for Jesus you are?"

By this point, I've realized what's happened: our campus—identified as a place touched by evil and in need of comfort—has become a setting where opportunistic young evangelists can come to save souls. My own uncle, the vice president of the Seventh-day Adventist church, had sent me an email the day before, telling me how proud he was of the church's response to the tragedy. This message had roused in me an indignant anger, and I'd fired off a hotheaded email to my unsuspecting mother, in which I typed the following rant: *What kind of world is he living in where he feels the need to express "pride" for booklets presented as self-help devices but that are actually SDA doctrine delivery devices? That really makes me angry. People are grieving here. Truly grieving. If he thinks this is a chance to indoctrinate people, he is truly out of touch with reality.*

I am less direct with the Jesus girl, and instead of delivering unto her a number that will qualify my on-fire-for-Jesus-ness, I say something dismissive, like, "That's irrelevant," a statement that reflects my inability, in the face of a young girl's unfathomable audacity, to communicate coherently.

A hundred yards later, we're interrupted by another woman. She's wearing a brown velour tracksuit. She has bleached blonde hair. Pink lips. Tan skin. A diamond dangles at her neck. She wants to know if we know for a fact that if we died today we would go to heaven.

What we tell her: "No, thanks."

*

Students—those who knew Cho, who knew of him, who lived with or near him—claim that they tried to befriend him. To greet him. To include him. Maybe they did. Maybe they didn't. Maybe they're saying this in order to evade responsibility, to make themselves feel better. "Hey," they think, "I tried saying hi to him, I tried talking to him and he wouldn't talk, he wouldn't speak." I wonder, though, if anyone called him out. If they were ever like "Hey, Cho, you know what? This whole ridiculous act you're putting on, this whole farcical, existential, I'm-tormented-and-won't-speak is total bullshit." Or what if someone had kept at it? Like really kept at it. Like dedicated themselves to being Cho's friend, really been like, "Hey, you know that guy who never speaks? I'm pouring all my energy into him, I'm going to make him better, and I'm going to say to him, you aren't unlovable, people don't hate you, they just maybe think you don't speak English, or that you're shy, or that you're psycho—are you psycho?—because it's okay to be psycho, as long as you don't hurt anybody or yourself. I'm going to love you if it kills me."

At noon the next day, hundreds of students and faculty—all wearing orange and maroon—stream into the Drill Field for a memorial service. A makeshift memorial in front of Burrus

Hall features thirty-two limestone slabs, each one piled with flowers and stuffed animals and candles and laminated photos: faces of the slain. Balloons—maroon and white and orange—are released; I watch them fly away, until they are tiny dots in the sky, until my brain is tricking me into thinking I still see them. A chaplain reads the full name of each victim, after which, a bell is rung. This happens thirty-two times. I lose count, think it's never going to end.

*

In my creative writing class, I ask how everyone's doing. Nobody responds. Hardly anybody ever responds when I ask that question, but today it seems worse because it is. People are quiet. People aren't talking. They aren't whispering, aren't chatting. A student named Ashley looks as if she's on the brink of tear-burst. I read something I'd written to start class. Not only does it feel inadequate, it's riddled with errors. I hadn't been able to see them until I started reading. In places, it literally makes zero sense. But maybe, I think, making zero sense is the kind of thing that needs to happen, the only thing that—in the wake of this terrible thing—can happen.

*

For weeks, our school exists at the epicenter of a place in history, a supercharged moment in an absurd world, a world whose semi trucks are delivering drawings from elementary schools, transporting shipments of teddy bears, handmade quilts, framed photographs, memorial ribbons, memory books, paper chains and paper cranes. Inside the Squires Student Center, the walls have been draped with plastic banners bearing the logos of other universities. They're like giant slippery flexible cards Sharpied with the names of well-wishers and people who are keeping Hokies in their thoughts and prayers. I pause to read some, wondering, "Do they mean me? Am I a Hokie?" Everybody from everywhere seems to be saying the same things to us, repeating the same chants: "We are keeping you in our thoughts and prayers" and "We are all Hokies today." I wonder who made these banners, what kind of person organizes or even knows to organize something like this—and why a banner and a sheet?—who has the energy and the unselfconsciousness and generosity to do such a thing, to write "We Will Prevail" and then sign one's name.

*

I go for a run. At the halfway mark I trip on a frost heave in the asphalt, fall, scrape the palms of my hands. The endorphins, the pain, the sight of blood—I don't know what else to do but brush myself off and keep running. The phrase *blood on my hands* appears in my mind. I'm afraid to wipe the blood on my sleeves, as I'm wearing my new Hokies shirt. I start to run, but I can't. I'm hyperventilating. I'm crying. It feels good. I'm sad when it passes. I would like to cry more, but my grief feels buried, a well that's too deep to tap into.

*

Undergraduates gather in Shanks—the name now suggests homemade weaponry—for treats: a plate of ham, finger sandwiches, Cokes, brownies. Nobody eats. A tall, angular professor hoists a tray and totes it around the room, accepting refusals of food with a gracious nod. Our famous poet sits at a table, signing copies of the poem she read at the convocation, copies of which the department is distributing to English majors. The line to get the poem signed leads out the door and down the hall. I ask Hannah, a former student, how she's doing. She rolls her eyes. "This sucks," she says. I ask if she's going to get her poem signed. "Yeah," she says, "I'm gonna be like, 'Will you sign my depressing keepsake?'" I laugh, but it's not funny. I still don't know what to do with the phrase *We will prevail*—a phrase that's already been transformed into signage, emblazoned upon the back windows of Blazers and Explorers and Range Rovers like so many talismans. I worry about the *we*. I worry it's not true. Would we *all* prevail? Maybe not. Certainly most would. Most needed to know that someone they loved and trusted believed they had the power to move on. Most needed to know this wouldn't happen again, that their school was still safe and fun and awesome, that it couldn't be changed, that the phrase *Virginia Tech* wouldn't only be a phrase that would resurrect the word *massacre*.

But what about the rest? What about the some? Because let's face it. Some got screwed. Some lost their one and onlys, their favorites. Some lost the loves of their lives, their fathers and mothers and brothers and sisters. Some will toil in darkness—for years—and never recover. Some can't—and won't—be inspired. The eyes of some won't get watery when ESPN plays lonely trumpet music over a montage of VT photos before sporting events, because they're not watching sporting events, especially not those that take place at Virginia Tech. Some see "NeVer ForgeT" bumper stickers and avert their eyes, because "never forget"—for some—sounds like a curse.

*

My son—three and a half years old—is asleep. My son, I'd like to report, has a cherubic face. Then again, most children do, especially when sleeping. Years before, I imagine, the parents of the slain gazed upon their own sleeping toddlers and presumed those faces to be cherubic. These parents reflected on the passage of time, acknowledged that their children would not always look like they looked now, secretly wished they wouldn't grow up, that they would always remain small enough to be held. They did not worry that these children would bleed to death on the floors of university classrooms. They did not imagine that their dying children would pretend to be dead, in the hopes that they might stay alive.

Someday, my son will ask about the shootings. Someday, he will enter *Virginia* and *Tech* into Google, or some other superpowered search engine, and it will automatically add *Massacre*. He will read the dates, do the math, realize he was alive and kicking not two miles away. He will have no memory of any of it, will not remember the time when his parents were glued to the television for hours on end, will have forgotten that his father became impatient when he clambered over him, how his father, when the shooter appeared on TV, guns pointed at the audience, shielded his eyes.

*

Two years after the shootings, a Chinese student will remove a knife from a backpack and decapitate another Chinese student, a woman, in a place called the Graduate Life Center. He will walk around Au Bon Pain holding up her head.

The year after that, two students—a young man and a young woman—will be shot fatally at Caldwell Fields, a meadow skirted by a creek about twelve miles from campus. There will be no witnesses. There will be no suspects. The murderer will not be apprehended.

Four and a half years later, I will receive an email from VT Alerts that says, "Gun shots reported—Coliseum Parking lot. Stay Inside. Secure doors. Emergency personnel responding. Call 911 for help." Despite the tone of the message—and despite the fact that I had been on campus during the shootings on April 16, 2007—I shrug it off. Six months before, students at a VT summer camp claimed they saw a man carrying a gun across campus. Nothing came of it. Furthermore, I am now accustomed to receiving emails from VT Alerts on a regular basis; they inform me of robberies and assaults—however few—that occur on Virginia Tech's campus.

So untroubled am I by reports of gunshots that I plan to go about my day, which involves driving to campus to meet a student in my office. I'm halfway there when my sister sends me a text message: "Are u okay? I heard there was lockdown there." I text back something sarcastic and dismissive. But after I park my car and as I begin walking toward Shanks, I realize that nobody's out, anywhere. Sure, it's Reading Day, but still. I slide out my phone, check my email. Another message from VT Alerts informs me that: "A police officer has been shot. A potential second victim is reported at the Cage lot. Stay indoors. Secure in place."

I reach my building. It's locked. I take out my keys, open the door, but can't get the key back out. I twist and turn and tug. I panic a little. It's exactly like the movies when the main character is trying to get the keys into the ignition but can't, and there's no explanation for why this one simple thing that should work, doesn't. After maybe thirty seconds, I retrieve the keys, ascend the stairs to my floor. All doors closed. I feel safer in my office, where I load Twitter and CNN. *Déjà vu*, I think. I can't believe this is happening. Again. It's two hours before my department chair knocks on my door, tells me it's safe to leave. A day will pass before we learn that the assailant was a Radford University student, and that he'd shot the policeman and, minutes later, himself.

*

I tell myself I remain untroubled. I do not seek counseling. I am not plagued by fear or nightmares. But I often imagine dying. I ride my bike on the Huckleberry Trail, see guys dressed vaguely like thugs or gangbangers, imagine them unzipping hoodies to reveal bandoliers, cocking Glocks, and blasting holes through my torso. I pass people on campus who look weird or unkempt or simply just mean, and I imagine them sliding firearms from their waistbands, spraying my brains against Hokie stone. But nobody does. For me, violence is an imaginary reconstruction, a sick fantasy I replay over and over, if only to prepare myself for the moment when it happens for real, and I can say, with some detachment, *This is exactly how I imagined it.*

*

There's a computer in the corner of the second floor of Virginia Tech's Newman Library reserved especially for those who wish to read official documents pertaining to the events of April 16, 2007. I'd considered visiting the terminal on a number of occasions, simply because I was curious about what, exactly, these documents might say, but the sign above the monitor, which announces that the computer is to be used only for accessing the special database, acted as much as a deterrent as advertisement, and for years, I was too sheepish to visit. I can't explain why, really, except maybe to say I had no "good" reason to do so and worried that anyone who saw me sitting there—in front of a screen that faces a corner, so as to guarantee privacy for its user—would attribute my browsing to some kind of morbid curiosity. I wondered if this designation had prevented others from visiting as well; I'd never seen anyone else accessing the database—that is, until I decided to visit the library with the sole intent of accessing it myself. It turned out that the person—a bearded man with glasses—who had parked himself before the monitor was not performing research; he was an employee updating security software. When I returned later to find the station vacant, I discovered that I could not access the database, in part because it required a login that I didn't have. I visited the information desk, summoned a librarian who led me back to the terminal, rifled through a few handouts in a plastic holder, but failed to find what he was looking for. In the end, he didn't know how to access it either. I mentioned that I'd never seen anybody using it, and he wasn't surprised; he hadn't been asked by anybody for the login in two years.

*

People will say, "So what's up with Blacksburg?" They will wonder—they will ask, point blank—if we're cursed. We—of all people—won't know. It will be difficult to persuade others that we aren't; we don't feel like we are. We live, we think, in a kind of paradise. In some ways, it is not so different from the world the Ingleses and other English settlers inhabited in the mid-eighteenth century, when they lived in Draper's Meadow. We have blue mountains and green hills. We see foxes under our overpasses; we discover deer grazing on our lawns. The world's second-oldest river flows through our county. We know and like and have genuine affection for our neighbors. We often leave our doors unlocked. Our children run through their yards, unsupervised, unimpeded, wild. We stand outside at night, under the stars, and despite all that has happened, and because it is something we are committed to feeling, we tell ourselves that we are safe, and that certainly, now, the worst of it must surely be over.

GHOST HOUSE

Once upon a time, there was a defense lawyer who was a member of the little church my family attended—a man who became a frequent visitor to our home. The defense lawyer was a few years younger than my parents—a big guy, but not fat, not skinny, not muscular. Just big, imposing, and strong. To be in a room with the defense lawyer was to experience the absolute fullness of his presence, which was embodied by the sonorous, rhythmic beat of his voice. The defense lawyer had survived polio as a child, and now with one bad leg limped with gusto through life, the motion of which caused his bangs to flop against his forehead. I'd known him most of my life and admired his sense of humor, which was brash and irreverent and cocky. He was the kind of guy who knew how to interact with kids, who paid them the kind of attention they loved, meaning that he knew how to be warmly adversarial. He seemed to legitimately enjoy making fun of me, and because he was smart and funny and ruthless, he made making fun of me *fun* for me. He got a kick out of reminding me about the time, for instance, that he flicked me, hard, on the knuckles. This had happened one evening when he'd stopped by, as he often did, for Friday night supper: I'd been banging on the piano and my mother, who had been in the kitchen preparing our food, yelled at me to stop, but like all juvenile dingbats who'd rather continue doing what they wanted to do instead of obeying their parents, I kept playing, who knows why, maybe because once I started a song, even as one as poorly composed as mine most likely was, I had a very strong compulsion to finish it, and so the defense lawyer, who was sitting on a nearby couch, reached over and flicked one of my hands, right on the knuckle. It surprised me, and it stung. It really hurt, actually, and this was part of the surprise: that a simple flick—like some kind of jujitsu technique the defense lawyer had, over the years, come to master—could inflict real pain. For a second, maybe a little while longer than a second, I resented him, in the way that I resented all adults who weren't my parents when they attempted to discipline me, but the defense lawyer just laughed when I said, "Hey, what'd you do that for?" and threatened to flick me again if I continued to disobey my mother's instructions. Pouting, I slunk away, which made him laugh. Of course, I couldn't hate him forever, partly because he was a great storyteller who told stories about what it was like to grow up in Michigan, a repertoire that included a story about how the boy's dean—now a retired pastor who led lively song services at our church—had cried when he'd found the defense lawyer and his friends playing cards on the Sabbath, and partly because it was the defense lawyer who would soon introduce me to the son of a woman the defense lawyer happened to be dating, a boy who would become, as the defense lawyer had predicted, my best friend. I'd heard about this boy long before I met him. The defense lawyer had assured me that we would get along great; after all, as he put it, we both "played with dolls." This was, as you might imagine, an assertion with which I took issue. The G. I. Joe figures I collected were not "dolls." They were "action figures." The defense lawyer disagreed. "So tell me," he'd say, "these little men you play with. They're not real, are they? They're little replicas of people, right? Isn't that what a doll is? So by definition, you'd have to admit that your little man there could be classified as a doll, right?" (The defense lawyer said, "Right?" a lot. It was a thing he did almost every time he made any kind of claim, which had the effect of making him seem both hesitant and assertive.) One Saturday, the defense lawyer brought his girlfriend and his girlfriend's kids to church. My best-friend-to-be showed up for Sabbath School—which was exactly like Sunday School only it happened on Saturdays—and in the room where my age group met, on a shelf in a closet, there was a box, a yellow cardboard container that, as far as I can remember, was used to collect money for some cause or other, probably something to do with evangelistic efforts or disaster relief or a mission field. My friend-to-be pointed at the box and immediately laughed and said, "Who is that gayblade?" I'd never heard anyone use the word *gayblade*, had no idea what it meant, only that it was most certainly derogatory and therefore did not belong in a Sabbath School classroom, where we would soon sing songs about loving Jesus and going to Heaven and hear stories about boys and girls doing good deeds or learning their lessons forevermore. I liked this boy immediately, which meant, of course, that the defense lawyer's prophecy had come true. The boy and I became instant friends, playing with our action figures and drawing comic books and riding our bikes through town and getting called "skaters" because of our quasi-angular haircuts. I started to visit the boy's house—a little white farmhouse with a green roof, whose address was 101 Oak Street. There was something quintessentially wholesome—if not downright American—even then, about a street named "Oak," something classical about the designation "101," a number that the defense lawyer's girlfriend had chosen herself, because once upon a time, the house had no number. It had no mailbox, which was fine, because the family lived within walking distance of the post office. Still, my friend's mother must have decided that houses were incomplete without a numeral signifying their place on the street, so she selected the digits from metal rungs at the Builder's Supply where, incidentally, she worked as a secretary, and nailed them to the front wall of the white, green-roofed structure where she and her kids lived, a house from whose windows you could see distant, pale blue mountains. I loved this house from the moment I met it, partly because it wasn't mine and almost all houses that weren't mine were somehow mysterious and exotic, especially those that were in actual neighborhoods, unlike mine, which sat at the bottom of a mountain on a little hill above two streams, and partly because it was the house where my friend lived: a goofy, bespectacled kid with a penchant for Chef Boyardee and toaster waffles and Intellivision and the Chicago Cubs. I loved it because it sat exactly one block away from Main Street in my hometown—a sad little grid of decaying brick buildings—which meant that my friend and his sister—a brunette who, though she was younger, was taller and who also enjoyed mocking the residents of our town using our own versions of their countrified twang—could exit their house and within minutes be inside the Piggly Wiggly, where a vast array of treats—chewing gum, candy, *MAD* magazines—awaited us. And so, in no time at all, the house at 101 Oak Street became my favorite destination, even if visiting it involved a ride on my bike that my mother wasn't crazy about, since doing so involved the navigation of windy back roads and crossing the four-lane highway that ribboned through the heart of our valley, and drivers could be crazy, plus my mom knew my friend's mother and the defense lawyer weren't always around, and that the boy and his sister and I would often have free reign of the house, and the idea of three kids playing without any "supervision" unnerved her. What she didn't know—and what my friend's mother and the defense lawyer kept absolutely secret—was that when the couple would say they had to run an errand, they would steal away for hours at a time to the man's cabin at the top of a nearby ridge—another exotic home that was, I knew, full of objects that invited introspection and pulsed with mystery: toothy geodes—like the cracked-open eggs of dragons—from the American southwest; a drawing, hung on the kitchen wall, of Jesus, whose closed eyes popped open if you stared long enough; a secret wall safe behind a tapestry; a wall-hung sword; a dead flying squirrel (which lived in the freezer); and the defense lawyer's record collection, which included the melancholy compositions of New Age harpist Andreas Vollenweider and the Beatles' *Sgt. Pepper's* album (my friend and I would look for Aleister Crowley on the cover because we'd both read a book called

Rock's Hidden Persuader, which had exposed various bands' attempts at so-called "backmasking," and the idea of musicians inserting secret backwards messages into their songs fascinated us). There, at this cabin, the defense lawyer and his girlfriend would smoke pot and have sex, and though neither of these activities seems especially scandalous to me now, back then the notion that the defense lawyer and my friend's mother had escaped so that they could fuck and do drugs would've absolutely blown our sweet little minds. We were good kids, after all, and my friend was far better than I ever wanted to be, meaning that he was more conscientious, and nearly impossible to tempt, and exceptionally stubborn in his refusal to break rules—especially those set by his mother. Aside from showing me a *Playboy* that had been stashed—presumably by the defense lawyer, but who knows—in his mother's closet, I remember my friend acting as our collective conscience, saying, if I suggested we should treat ourselves to another Little Debbie, that, "No, mom wouldn't want that," a phrase that, as soon as he uttered it, indicated that whatever plan, with whatever rule I'd proposed we break, was now as good as dead. And so, and in these ways, 101 Oak Street became my second home. It was the place where we ate grilled cheese sandwiches in the wooden booth of a breakfast nook and listened to a silver boom box that played cassettes of Hall & Oates and Michael Jackson and the Beatles and 10,000 Maniacs, stuff my parents would have never played, because they didn't listen to rock, only gospel and easy listening. A place where my friend and I held our breath whenever the defense lawyer's boxer—who spent most of her time in this house—emitted her silent but deadly farts.

Where, because I could never master the track pad, I ended up spending hours watching my friend play Intellivision, navigating the mazes of Dungeons and Dragons and shooting arrows at snakes, which, once hit, dispersed into digital mist. Where we watched the defense lawyer's boxer nurse a litter of puppies and where the defense lawyer knelt down and, taking one of the dog's wrinkly teats—it looked like a miniature sausage link—between his fingers, he squeezed, thereby lasering a thread of dog milk into his open mouth, for no other reason than to gross us out. Where the house's single toilet had a wooden lid and on the bathroom wall a photo of nineteenth-century lumberjacks circling a giant redwood with axes and a caption that said, "Small strokes fell great oaks." Where we watched Cubs games on WGN and laughed at the voice of Harry Caray. Where, outside in the street, we played keep-away from the boxer, whose frothing saliva would beslime the ball we threw. Where we watched MTV and made fun of any singer who took themselves too seriously, especially Bruce Springsteen. Where I'd stand on Saturday mornings, waiting for my friend to get dressed in the light of *Transformers* or *He-Man*, the forbidden shows of Saturday morning, shows I had never before seen, not on Saturday, a day that the majority of American kids, I knew, spent glazed by the lurid glow of Hanna-Barbera cartoons, slurping milk sugared by the same rainbow-colored cereals that were advertised during the toon's commercial breaks. Then: to church, where on the rare occasion we'd be allowed to sit together, we'd crack each other up with the sketches we drew onto the backs of a church bulletin, each taking turns to create an outlandish toon-scape, a veritable Boschian garden of absurdist delight. Or this: us at a sleepover, laughing hysterically at the fart noises we made by squishing our cupped palms underneath our armpits or blowing on the flesh of our forearms, while outside my friend's window, his mother and the defense lawyer giggled at the thought of us giving ourselves over, so purely, to laughter. Or this, much later, after we'd gone off to college: my friend's mom and the defense lawyer finally, after eight years of dating, getting married, selling the white farmhouse with the green roof, and moving to Collegedale, Tennessee, home of Southern Missionary College and the Little Debbie factory. And finally: six months after the wedding, a separation, instigated by the defense lawyer, who simply decided to up and leave, and who subsequently filed for divorce. A few years passed, I graduated from boarding school, went to college, graduated, returned home, and needed a job, so I agreed to work for a time for the defense lawyer, who needed someone to fill in during maternity leave for his secretary, a vivacious blond who dialed phones faster than anyone I'd witnessed previously, and who, before she left, taught me how to type complaints and emergency custody orders that the defense lawyer dictated onto little cassettes. It was around this time that the defense lawyer began corresponding with a woman in California, a woman who was very pretty but, in my estimation, not very bright, and who, in the end, became enamored with the defense lawyer, who asked for her hand in marriage. The two were married very quickly and the woman from California moved into the cabin, whose interior she subsequently and single-handedly transformed, a process that involved the removal of the wall-hung sword and the magic Jesus poster and the glittering toothy geodes, replacing all this with decorative plates and hand-sewn quilts and a portrait of a guardian angel protecting two children as they crossed a rickety bridge in the night. Despite this massively thorough overhaul, the defense lawyer and his new wife did not live in the cabin much longer; eventually, they migrated to the Pacific Northwest, where the defense lawyer became a prosecutor, and then, after a time, a judge. I still talk to my friend—he lives in Finland now, with two kids and a wife who's pursuing a postdoc in linguistics—but it's been a long time—over a decade—since I've spoken to the defense lawyer. Even so, I have, upon returning to my hometown, visited 101 Oak Street, and am sad to report that the little white farmhouse with a green roof no longer lives at such location. In fact, the house itself is completely gone, as if it somehow vanished, or got up and walked away. Furthermore, absolutely no evidence—no ditch or foundation of any kind—exists to suggest that anything or any human had ever lived there, or that anything I claimed to have experienced in such a house had been anything but a dream: only a green field remains, flush with swishing grass. Which means, of course, that the only people who can still see the house are the ones who have seen it before, and the ones who can see it the best—with the most clarity, and with the pang that accompanies the recollection of a home that has disappeared—no longer live here, and are not likely ever to return.

THE OTHER, INVENTED MAN

For many years—the majority of my life, in fact—acknowledging death's inevitability exerted little psychological pressure on me. I had no fear of passing, as they say, from this world into the next, or, assuming no next world exists, simply entering oblivion. I often reminded myself of something the acclaimed Buddhist writer Alan Watts had said, which is that none of us can remember our birth, and neither will we remember our death, so what do we really have to fear? I'd become less sure than I had been in my youth about the possibility of an afterlife—even the word *afterlife* made less sense to me, because I could not separate life from consciousness, and consciousness was everything to me. For years I had been telling myself that I would rather die "early" than recede into mental and/or physical decrepitude, but I hadn't—at least, not until recently—acknowledged that even though the bodily "me" would continue to morph and change, decaying with time, breaking down, acquiring new flaws that wouldn't simply go away but would have to be dealt with, the interior "me" would stay more or less the same, the illusion of continuous identity over time being perhaps the most powerful and convincing trick that the mind plays on us.

But lately my thinking about death had become so pervasive that I'd begun to see it everywhere. The books I read and the television shows I watched and the songs I sang along to on the radio nearly all dealt, in either oblique or straightforward ways, with human mortality, and in the evenings, after making dinner for my family and cleaning up and taking the dog for her evening constitutional, I often played a video game in which I guided my avatar around city streets, killing people and evading police until the green bar indicating how much "life" I had left grew short, then turned red, then disappeared altogether.

No activity, though, inspired thoughts of my own imminent demise as much as riding a bicycle. I'd been riding regularly for six years but only recently had graduated from car-free greenways to rural back roads, and when I described my usual route to friends and colleagues, they often expressed dismay. I got it. I, too, once would have thought it nothing less than a suicide mission to ride my bike on a narrow, curving road where jacked-up dual-cab pickup trucks hauling trailers would blow past me on blind corners. Though I rationalized that the road was popular with cyclists and that the vast majority of motorists, even if they were speeding, were aware of this fact, I used the occasion of every car approaching me from the rear to envision that today was the day I'd be knocked off my bike or simply plowed over, and then, due to devastating injuries to my physical self, the thought-producing and sensation-generating entity that pulsed so wondrously at the center of my being would dissolve.

In the past, whenever I'd had occasion to confront the fact of my limited existence, I would try to comfort myself by acknowledging that I had already lived "long enough." It wasn't that I wanted to die right now, or even within the next twenty or thirty years, but I could reflect on the life I'd lived and consider it full. I'd grown up in the verdant mountains of the American Southeast, survived a strict-but-loving religious upbringing, fallen in love, had my heart broken, traveled abroad and within the United States, married, fathered a child, moved to a college town in the mountains of Virginia, taught classes, written books, hosted parties, and posted photos of extraordinary sunsets and failed basketball trick shots and local waterfalls to my preferred social media site. I suspected that, unless I contracted some painful disease, I would never actually want to die and be ferried off to heaven, or to hell, or to become a ghost haunting the world, or to simply disappear.

I couldn't think of myself dying without thinking about my wife and son and the effect it would have on their lives. I didn't know if my wife would remarry, but I found myself hoping that she would find someone, a man a few years older, perhaps: successful, wealthy but not incredibly so, active, handsome. I found it strangely comforting to imagine her, after my untimely passing, cohabitating with someone she loved and who took care of her needs; a man who knew his way around the kitchen, and how to clean, and—not insignificantly—was a safe driver, as my wife did not appreciate when I drove fast or recklessly, or even semi-fast or semi-recklessly, and was made intensely uncomfortable by the application of the gas pedal to the floorboard, no matter what the reason.

I had not played this little game before—of imagining the particular characteristics of the man my widowed wife might marry. Far more familiar to me was the exercise in which I imagined my wife had died, leaving me to find a new partner, which I had convinced myself I would eventually do, even if it meant settling—as it certainly would—for someone I loved less.

Part of me wishes that I couldn't imagine being married to anyone but my wife, but I can, because it is my business as a writer to imagine, and because I have spent the better part of my life daring myself to consider the so-called unimaginable. Furthermore, I spent my youth imagining who, in the future, might end up becoming the love of my life. I often stood in the hallway of the house where I grew up, a corridor whose walls were hung with framed pictures and where it was normally so dark that I had to switch on an overhead light to study images of my mother and father on their wedding day, after which I would ask my mother to take down the music box—a glossy, polished container whose lid I liked to open so I could watch the gears rotate as they plinked out "Clair de Lune," the song my mother said was "their" song. I wanted a song. I wanted a wife. I wanted a wedding and a reception where I fed said wife cake. And for the first quarter-century of my life, every girl I found myself attracted to auditioned for that role—if only in my head.

I feel compelled to say now that I would never leave my wife, not even in my fantasies. And since I would not leave her, I had to imagine conditions that would allow, with conclusive verisimilitude, this new story line to exist. The easiest, most plausible way for this to happen was for my wife to die. It turned out this was easy to imagine. I'd been imagining the deaths of people I've loved for as long as I could remember. As a kid, when one or both of my parents failed to return home on time, I would gaze out our living-room window into the dark yard and the even darker woods beyond, and a voice inside me would say, *They're dead. Your parents are dead. Gone forever. And now you're an orphan. You'll have to live somewhere else now, with someone else.* And I'd imagine being shipped off to Africa—specifically to Abidjan, Ivory Coast, where my aunt and uncle, who were to raise my sister and me in the case of our parents' deaths, lived. I'd have to share space with my three younger girl cousins and live in a house surrounded by a wall and guarded by a man named Mohammed, who had once been called upon to machete to death a black mamba in their yard.

As harrowing as it was to imagine my wife dying—leaving our son inconsolable and his father helpless in a house whose every surface had the power to summon her ghost—I had to admit that it was stimulating to think of reentering the dating world in middle age, joining matchmaking websites, and swiping through profiles on my phone. Perhaps, to lessen the anguish of my wife's passing, I would gorge myself on the thrill of meaningless sexual encounters in a way that I never actually had when single, having never either enjoyed or regretted a one-night stand.

What might these other women ask of me? Would I attend one of those new fundamentalist churches that had verbs for names, like "Arise" or "Emerge" or "Transform," and that advertised good coffee and rock music and were led by a team of young pastors with tattoos who cursed when appropriate and wore stylish, ragged clothes and headset mics when they preached? Could I become a CrossFit demagogue? A vegetarian? A Unitarian? The only thing I knew was that I would have to become someone else. The me I was now—predicated as it was on my proximity to my wife and her needs, so many of which I failed to meet— would come to seem alien. If I stared at a woman long enough, no matter who, scenes of possible futures would flash through my brain. If I let any one scenario play out, however, I always foresaw complications—the main one being that none of these new women I might somehow convince to go out with me and possibly to share a bed with me was my wife. My wife, I needed to remember, was exceptional, and it was for this very reason that I'd married her. Strong, reasonable, employing common sense at every turn, a powerhouse of knowledge, capable of seeing through whatever bullshit persona another human attempted to execute, beautiful but not obsessed with her appearance, quick to anger but quicker to apologize, she was—at her very core—a loving, funny, kind, softhearted woman, content with the simple pleasures of good food and good drink, a clean house, a back rub, a hug, an evening stroll, an absorbing mystery to watch before bed, a good night's rest, and a new rug for the living room.

*

If, on the other hand, I died first and my wife remarried, it was easy to imagine that the man she might end up with would be a kind of upgrade. Maybe this new guy—who appeared not too soon after my untimely passing but sooner than my wife had ever allowed herself to imagine—would be the kind of person who, like her, had lost one or both parents too early and could therefore commiserate, or, more likely, understand the need *not* to commiserate, because, for the most part, details and stories about long-dead parents need not be dwelled upon. Maybe my wife and this new guy would share other things in common: an impulse to always turn the radio volume down a few notches; a disdain for cold cheese of any variety; a deep suspicion of CrossFit enthusiasts; a lack of desire to sign up for a yoga class, regardless of how transformative their friends promised it would be. This new guy, I surmised, would enjoy exercising but not necessarily need to go for long hikes in the woods, which were full of spiderwebs and poison-secreting plants and stinging insects—unless, that is, my wife were to develop a sudden yearning to experience some particular wilderness, which most likely she wouldn't, as she's always been content to walk through the neighborhood where we lived and where we recently purchased what she jokingly refers to as our "forever home," meaning that, if all goes according to plan, we will grow old and die in this house. Though perhaps if I happen to croak unexpectedly, she might feel the need to move on, if only to get away from the rooms that reminded her so much of me. Of course, it's also possible that if the new guy bought her a rug for the living room and finally purchased some decent furniture for the master bedroom—as my wife and I have talked many times about doing, looking online at various configurations of dressers, beds, bedside tables, and wardrobes but never seeming to be able to decide on anything in the end and so making do with the old-but-serviceable furnishings we've been living with for more than a decade—then maybe, perhaps almost certainly, she could begin a new life in the same house.

There was something pleasurable in thinking about this other, invented man, for to imagine a man who was not me, but who had won my approval and favor, necessitated that I assign to him the very attributes that I myself lacked. I supposed, for instance, that this new man wouldn't snore, or, if he did, he'd figure out a solution rather than outright denying that it ever happened. Unlike me, the new guy would be good with his hands, able to fix anything that breaks, generous, doting, but not so much as to smother her with unwanted affection. Despite an appreciation for music of all kinds, including whatever pop confection happened to pour out of the car radio thanks to my son's love of the local Top 40 station, the new guy would not be into music *too* much; would never waste time searching for rare LPs online; would not secretly drop two hundred bucks at a time buying vinyl on eBay. Maybe he'd be able to play a few songs on the piano or guitar, but he wouldn't have aspirations to be in a band or someday cut an album. In fact, this other, invented man would be burdened with few aspirations, aside from making enough money to pay the bills and set aside a decent amount for retirement, and attending to the needs of my wife and son, and maybe gardening or, better, learning his way around the kitchen until he could bake gluten-free cakes and breads that no one, least of all my wife, could tell were flourless.

Needless to say, this new man would not play video games for hours in front of the downstairs TV or have a juvenile affinity for hooded sweatshirts, except maybe in the mornings, in lieu of a robe, though I could definitely see him being the robe-wearing type. And it was clear to me that—robe or no—he would never stick his head into a room where my wife was working and suggest that it might be a good time to join him in bed, or ask point-blank if she might want to join him in the removal of his clothes, because even though this guy—the new one, I mean—would be in possession of a profound libido, he would also have vast reserves of patience, and would go to workmanlike lengths to keep said libido in check, and would never suggest, except through his unwavering ability to put my wife first in all things, that he was the least bit interested in sex. He'd never try to steer a casual hug into something more amorous; never raise his eyebrows in a comically suggestive way; never purposefully walk past her in his underwear with a morning erection, as if this sign of virility would stir her to action, regardless of how often this same effort had failed in the past, and though he might seem indifferent, as soon as the woman suggested that now might be a good time to have sex, he would be instantaneously ready to go.

I imagined, too, that the new guy would be the sort to take care of himself. He would not drink excessively, would not guzzle a pre–five-o'clock cocktail before my wife returned home, for fear that she might observe, accurately, that he was drinking too much. The new guy would not sneak cigarettes after everyone had gone to bed or smoke pot from a blown-glass pipe tucked away in the garage. The new guy would also never intentionally inflict any sort of surprise upon my wife, who is easily startled and therefore does not think it's funny when someone creeps up on her and lightly touches her shoulder and says, "Boo!" Such a thing would never even occur to the new guy, who would not delight in antagonism of any kind, and would certainly not ever take the gong that was hanging in the downstairs office and sneak up behind my son while he was playing video games and bang it as hard as he could, creating a sound that would permeate the boy's body, flooding him with a kind of aural pain and causing him to erupt into tears and causing the woman to come downstairs, for she, too, had been disturbed by the shock of its sudden loudness.

This new guy—this other, invented man—would not lose his mind when my son confessed that he had forgotten the passcode to his phone and had locked himself out of the device, an act that would necessitate a two-hour search for instructions on how to restore the phone without erasing any important data. This invented man could handle such a quest without temper tantrums, which meant that my wife would have no legitimate reason to hurl sarcastic barbs and remind him that his own father would not have behaved this way, and how once he—the man—had forgotten to bring his computer home from college during spring break and his own father had made the ten-hour round trip to retrieve it. This other, invented man would not fling his hands up whenever he found himself behind slow drivers or stuck for longer than he would like at a red light because he, the new guy, would—as previously mentioned—have vast, inexplicable reserves of patience; would not only exemplify the kind of unflappability that few dads can ever be said to possess, but would also share with my son the methods he employed to control his temper and thus serve as an agent of tranquility.

It occurred to me that I might write a story about this other, invented man, casting him as somebody that I— or the narrator of my story—would eventually meet: a fellow professor, perhaps, or a doctor of some variety, an orthodontist or general practitioner. Perhaps the narrator of this story might have reason to make a visit to his primary care provider, just to make sure none of his minor afflictions—an unidentified rash, say, or a recently smashed thumbnail—were in fact serious. There, because the narrator's regular doctor, a plump, Christ-loving fellow who'd once likened smoking a single cigarette to hitting one's hand with a hammer, was on vacation, he would be seen by a new guy. An affable newcomer, this substitute, would ask the narrator what he did for exercise, and the narrator would say, "A little cycling" and "the occasional racquetball match," and the new doc might respond favorably, saying, "That's great. I'm a big cycling and racquetball fan myself," and the narrator would file that away, thinking, *Maybe I should invite him out for a ride or a game*, subsequently striking that from his thoughts, as it would seem too forward, and probably there was some kind of ethical standard the narrator couldn't quite put his finger on that legislated that doctors and patients were not to fraternize in such a way, but then the new guy would keep showing up in real life: the narrator would run into him at a matinee at the downtown movie theater, and they'd strike up a friendly conversation, or the narrator would see him at the Episcopal church he and his wife occasionally attended, and tap him on the shoulder during coffee hour and would make some lame joke, like, "We have to stop meeting like this," or "Come here often?" and the two men would make a date to ride Clover Hollow Trail or meet at War Memorial Gym on campus for a racquetball or pickup basketball game, and eventually the narrator would introduce the new guy to his wife, and the two would immediately hit it off. Maybe they'd grown up in the same county in North Carolina, attended the same high school, or both run cross-country at competing schools—after all, the world was so small that such things weren't inconceivable. Hadn't the narrator and his wife attended the same university as undergrads, majored in the same subject, never once meeting until after they'd both graduated, at which point they reminisced about teachers they'd shared or bars they'd frequented and even the same R.E.M. concert they'd attended, all without knowing the other? It was easy for me, the author of this tale, to imagine them—the narrator and his wife—taking interest in this other man, inviting him to dinner, plying him with cocktails to get his life story, which would, of course, include a tragedy of some kind, a partner or girlfriend or spouse who had recently passed away, maybe the other man's now-dead wife, like the friend of the narrator's own wife, had once been pregnant, but complications had arisen, and whatever caused the baby to die also caused the mother to die, and the narrator and his wife would say, "We are sorry, so sorry to hear such a thing," and the other man would get sad but then apologetically brush away his tears and ask for another glass of whatever he was having, just a splash more, and find an affable way to change the subject, and later, after he'd left and the narrator and his wife were cleaning up together, they'd plot to figure out whether they knew anyone to set this guy up with, he was so nice, after all, and so talented, not knowing, of course, that the narrator was on his last legs, that he had no more than six months, a year maybe, and that it would be the exact same man who would diagnose the narrator with whatever illness he'd contracted, and who would refer him to an oncologist or a particular surgeon, and in the narrator's eventual passing my wife would end up turning to the new guy, at first in grief, then in passion, and in the end the narrator would reveal himself, now a ghost, to have been dead the whole time, attempting to convince the reader that, by having lovingly penned this very story, that he was not—nor ever could be—jealous.

Though I never actually wrote such a story, I continued to conjure the narrator in my mind, and so familiar did he become that I began to fantasize that I might very well run into him in real life, at the grocery store, say, or on the street, at the farmers' market, or a local eatery or watering hole. It became a kind of secret and not unsatisfactory game for me: whenever I left the house, I found myself looking for this other man, taking as the premise that if I could imagine him with such clarity, he—or a version of him—might actually appear somewhere, even in my own backyard, that he might show up, for instance, as a referee of one of my son's soccer matches: a fit, older man who wouldn't shy away from red carding one of the opposing players, who, despite the fact that they were bigger and stronger, frequently lacked the necessary finesse and technical skills required to maintain possession of the ball and so would express their frustrations with shoves and sloppy tackling. And the more I watched him, the more convinced I would become that he was the other man—the one I had thought to have invented.

It occurred to me just now that it would please me immensely to say, after that last paragraph, "but then I actually *did* see him," or "I thought I saw him," or "I saw what I wanted to think was him," followed by a description of how I found a photo one day, that I'd opened an old poetry anthology from college, and an old Polaroid fell out, one that was slightly blurry and faded from age and that depicted my long-lost friend Amy, a fellow English major and writer who was grinning theatrically and posing beside a man asleep on a couch, a man whose face had been covered in magic marker, a man who, the longer I studied his face, the more familiar he became. Even so, no matter how long I stared, I had no way of retrieving his name, until eventually it hit me, like the beam of a flashlight in an otherwise pitch-black room, that this was he, this was the other man, I was sure of it, even chuckled at the idea that the other man would have been the kind of guy who fell asleep at parties, since my wife, who had often talked about the way her college friends had poked fun at her uncanny ability to nod off—after a few drinks—in public places, and that imagining them both doing this at the same time in their lives would be something that they would be able to reminisce fondly about. But then, when I turned the photograph sideways, and got a better look, I realized that there was a reason I recognized the other man, because the other man was me—but that didn't happen, either: I made that story up, too.

The only thing that I can say for sure about what happened is this: I invented another man, and now—as far as I can say—he's here to stay. And although I'd like to report otherwise, little has changed since he first made himself known. I wake, read all the news fit to print about our ailing democracy, greet my family, pour myself coffee, take note of the sun cresting above the ridges behind our house, marveling that I did not expire in my sleep, that here I am, for now, to greet another day, to find ways both to adore and disappoint those I love and—thus—to continue being myself. The spirit of the other, invented man lives on inside me, and somehow I find his presence, as absurd as it must surely sound, to be a comfort. He is, of course, a mere projection, a fantasy, but I've convinced myself that he is a possibility, a potential energy that lives for now inside the coffin of my body—neither living nor dead— and though he may expire when I do, these words here will be waiting—perhaps in vain, but perhaps not—for him to someday discover, assuming he might have cause someday to paw through my personal effects, since I well know that the ephemera of once-living people live a brief afterlife in the purgatories of closets and attics, and thus the other man might, in this way, discover this thing that I'm just now finishing, and hopefully he will recognize it as a kind of contract between him and me, or at the very least, a benediction, one that might enable him to go forth with courage and gratitude, living out the remainder of his life on Earth, knowing that I had somehow foreseen his coming and granted him, however feebly, my every blessing.

MUSIC OF THE SPHERES:
A MEDITATION ON NASA'S
SYMPHONIES OF THE PLANETS

*The knower of the mystery of sound knows the
mystery of the whole universe.*

—Hazrat Inayat Khan

I.

Upon first listening to NASA's *Symphonies of the Planets*, you
might find it difficult to hear any music at all. In fact, even
if you listen closely, you may hear only noise. Gurgling.
Static. Wobbling whistles. Rumblings. Bellowing. Wind-like
screeches. Droning undercurrents. Faint reverberations,
ringing like lost and lonely signals. The moan of what
sounds like—but is certainly not—a choir of human voices
singing indifferently. You might close your eyes and think of
wind tunnels and glacial caves and avalanches and oceans
and boiling mud pots. You might think of Earth noises. Of
Earth events. I doubt very much that you would, if asked to
guess the origins of these sounds, say the name of any other
planet in our solar system but ours. But it is our neighboring
planets—and their magnetospheres and radio waves—that
are responsible for these sounds. On this album, they are the
musicians.

II.

I loved white noise long before I knew what exactly to call it. As a kid, my bedroom window looked out onto our backyard. Just beneath the window an enclosure—a brown fence with a latched door—had been built, and inside it lived several garbage cans, a rhododendron, and the condenser unit for our central air system. I had gazed into this strange little enclosure many times as a child, watching the leaves of the rhododendron flap in the wind generated by the compressor, the sound of which had over the years become a sort of lullaby. On the evenings when I was sent to bed before the sun had set, I would lie there, staring at my ceiling, where a series of stretched and elongated shapes resembled the spear-carrying picadors I remembered from the book *Ferdinand the Bull*, only the figures on my ceiling appeared to be riding misshapen horses with extravagantly elongated legs, as if they were the cousins of Salvador Dali's elephants. This, and the fact that the riders were colorless, lent them a phantasmagoric effect, as if I were staring at a zombie bullfighter parade. The compressor would begin to whir, and I'd shut my eyes and fall asleep, to dream about earthly things.

III.

Something else I have always loved: space. I love stargazing. I love old footage of Buzz Aldrin walking on the moon. I love glow-in-the-dark stars and astronaut ice cream and constellations and the horsehead nebula and futurist depictions of spaceports and even the long, slow, boring parts of *2001: A Space Odyssey*. So as a junior at the University of North Carolina—an English major who needed a science course—I figured signing up for Astronomy 101 was a no-brainer. I attended the class regularly and took copious notes on everything from the Greek celestial sphere to the difference between hot and cold dark matter. I illustrated my transcriptions with doodles of the space shuttle, Galileo peering through a telescope, the starship *Enterprise*, cross-sections of planets, sketches of the sun's magnetic field, and a flowchart illustrating potassium argon dating. I learned that hotter light creates a bluer spectrum and cooler light creates a redder one, and that the stars in the sky are not fixed but moving away from us. I learned that astronomers constructed the story of our universe by studying the wavelengths and frequencies of light (which is itself an electromagnetic wave) and that when we lift our heads to the night sky, we bear witness to light that's billions of years old and that we are, therefore, gazing into the distant past.

It was the spring of 1995, the second semester of my first year as a transfer student at UNC. And because I'd spent my entire education in Seventh-day Adventist institutions, it was also my first year—at age twenty—of public school. Though I'd stopped going to church and had grown out my hair and smoked cigarettes and drank beer and ingested my fair share of mind-altering substances, I still refused to work on Saturday, because I believed it was the day that God had hallowed, the day on which he had rested during Creation Week. And as much as I enjoyed learning about stars and planets, I was troubled when my T.A. claimed that scientists basically had no choice but to conclude that our universe had begun as a hot, dense singularity—a uniform soup of subatomic particles and radiation. I also wasn't crazy about the prophecy he'd made concerning our sun: that one day it would balloon into a red giant so enormous it would absorb the Earth. Then again, I'd never questioned the creation story I'd been told, or the idea in the future of a world made new. Back at my parents' house, on my bedroom wall, hung a picture of a bearded man in a white robe and sash floating in space, his hands lovingly cradling Earth. This image had never struck me as odd or absurd. I did not think, *Why does this Creator have a nose when there's no air to breathe in space?* I did not think, *His fingers are the size of Argentina, so how is he going to fashion humans out of dirt?* Honestly, I can't remember what I thought, except that it was comforting to imagine that the benevolent and omnipotent deity watching over Earth took the form of a giant human being.

One day, during his office hours, I paid a visit to my T.A.—a sprightly young man with red hair and a beard— and asked him, point-blank, if he believed in God. He said he didn't. I asked why not. He said, "Because I only believe in things I can see."

I'm not sure what I wanted him to say. I would have appreciated it if he'd explained how a person could believe in a Creator while also accepting the conclusions that science had reached through the study of observable phenomena. But he hadn't. And so I walked away feeling a little bit superior (I knew that faith was, as Hebrews 11:1 says, "the substance of things hoped for, the evidence of things not seen") and a little bit troubled, because I worried that the people in charge of studying our universe had banished God from the cosmos.

IV.

My T.A. never played NASA's *Symphonies of the Planets* in Astronomy 101. Never mentioned them. I wish he would've. Fifteen years later, on the day I discovered the *Symphonies*, I listened all day and into the night, thinking, *Where has this been all my life?* My fascination with the album was immediate and palpable and quickly morphed into a full-blown obsession. I listened while doing the dishes. I listened while writing and reading. I listened while lacing up my boots and donning a coat and face gear and hooking the dog's collar to a leash and leading her outside, into the wind and snow. I listened as I drove, which made my car seem like a rover on an alien planet, and the streets and fields and houses I passed like improbable structures in another world. The *Symphonies* had me hypnotized. Elevated. Weirded out. Dazed. I felt as though I'd dialed in to an unsolvable mystery. Like I was carrying, between my ears, the secret heartbeat of the universe.

V.

The word *symphony* is a word whose Greek heritage likely summons associations of antiquity. The word from which it derives can be translated into "agreement or concord of sound." No doubt it calls to mind the most sophisticated genres of music, the kind played in concert halls by tuxedoed musicians. Deliberate. Complex. Painstakingly crafted. Not stuff produced by balls of gas and rocks orbiting a giant sphere of plasma.

I suppose you could make the argument that using the word *symphony* to describe these sounds is ultimately misleading. A symphony is—first of all—intentional.

There's intelligence behind a symphony. In other words, a symphony is not accidental. I think of other intelligent nonhumans that could be said to sing: monkeys, birds, certain breeds of dog. I suppose you could also call the singing of whales a symphony. You'd be wrong then, too, but you'd be less wrong.

Simply put: the symphonies of the planets are not symphonies.

They are sounds borne from chaos.

VI.

I like to pretend I'm not afraid of chaos. But like most people I know, I prefer predictability to randomness. The problem is: most events in life aren't foreseeable. For instance, we didn't ask to be born, but here we are. And we're all going to die someday, but none of us knows when. Disorder seems to be as much a part of our world as stability. And we all have ways of dealing with the predicament of our existence: we sing, pray, drink, dance, play, weep, work ourselves to the bone. We attend church on days we've deemed holy. We refuse to wash our jerseys after a win. We say "Bless you" when our neighbor sneezes. We knock on wood.

In short, we all have our rituals: the things we do to psyche ourselves out and to deliver the impression—if only for a moment—that we're in control. It's why I hold my breath when traveling through a tunnel or cross my fingers and toes when a Tarheel basketball player shoots a free throw. It's also why, when I'm stuck in a rut, or suffering a bout of anxiety, I don headphones and crank up the *Symphonies* and stare at the trees outside my office window. More often than not, this has the transformative effect of focusing the bedlam of my consciousness squarely on the present moment. For a little while, I'm not mired in the past. I'm not anxious about the future. I am in my body in the world, fully inhabiting the present, utterly mystified by existence, astonished and grateful to be here.

VII.

It's important for me to remain in the present. I have a tendency to drift. I spent my youth believing that I was responsible for knowing the origins—and the ultimate fate—of the entire universe. I thought about Creation Week a lot, because my family believed that the day we attended church—Saturday, which we called the Sabbath—had been set apart by God as a day of rest, in part to commemorate His own rest after having spent six days making the world, which had been flawless until Satan came along and messed it up. Then Jesus came and lived a perfect-example life and died for our sins, and if we accepted him as our Savior we would be taken to heaven with him at the End of Time. Satan would be destroyed. The books—the ones that Recording Angels had been writing and that recorded every human's actions—would be opened, God would be vindicated, and the universe's perfection would be restored.

A good Adventist kid would've spent more time in the Word. He would've listened only to sacred or classical music. He would've shunned TV and movies and books written by non-Adventists. He certainly wouldn't have transferred to a state university, to study English—a major that allowed me to gorge on electives.

Astronomy wasn't the only course that challenged my beliefs. In Intro to Philosophy, an Israeli professor led the class in an investigation of the concept of identity, interrogating the possibility of a person surviving one's death. In a Milton course piloted by a young professor who was so animated I imagined he'd snorted a line of coke before every class period, I encountered a writer who seemed more passionately connected to God than anyone I've ever met. I read Saussure and Lacan and Derrida and acknowledged that language—like any system of symbols—is a fluid, evolving medium and that universal truth is hard to come by. I read Wallace Stevens and had to agree with his observation that "death is the mother of beauty." I read the *Tao Te Ching* and thought, *Wow, these verses are as beautiful and true as anything I've read in the Old or New Testament.* And on a warm spring day, I was approached by a shaggily bearded young man—a kid who seemed to be wearing his entire wardrobe as a way to carry it with him—who had left his home and given up everything to spread the Gospel and was now asking me if I wanted to talk about the Bible. Moved by his earnestness, I asked him how he interpreted Revelation, thinking he might have a different key to unlock that inscrutable book. Instead he said, "I'm a babe in Christ, man. And Revelation, that's a piece of steak. You wouldn't feed steak to a baby, would you?"

In short: my world got complicated. And like a red giant, it began its slow and inevitable expansion.

VIII.

My friend Aaron—a poet and editor who owns a vast collection of LPs, many of them reissues of '80s new wave bands—was the first person to tell me about the *Symphonies*. Aaron knows that I like The Cure and New Order and The

Smiths. He also knows that I have, for many years, loved a genre of music called "space rock." According to Allmusic. com:

> The term *space rock* was originally coined back in the '70s to describe the cosmic flights of bands like Pink Floyd and Hawkwind. Today, however, *space rock* refers to a new generation of alternative/indie bands that draw from psychedelic rock, ambient music, and—more often than not—experimental and avant-garde influences. Space rock is nearly always slow, hypnotic, and otherworldly; it typically favors lengthy, mind-bending sonic explorations over conventional song structures, and vocals sometimes play second fiddle to the shimmering instrumental textures. Some space rock groups are explicitly drug-inspired, which makes sense given the typically narcotic effect of the style's foundation: washes of heavily reverbed guitar, minimal drumming, and gentle, languid vocals.

"Slow." "Hypnotic." "Otherworldly." "Shimmering instrumental textures." NASA's *Symphonies* bear a striking resemblance to the bands working the more abstract end of the space rock spectrum. These songs would be at home on Darla Records, an American independent record company and curator of the Bliss Out series, which the label describes as an opportunity for bands and artists "to step off their career path and showcase their musical Om." What this means exactly remains undefined, if rather unclear, though the series title suggests that its records might deliver to the listener a kind of ecstatic, even mystical experience. At the very least, the albums might be used for relaxation purposes: for years, I put myself to sleep by playing Windy and Carl's *Antarctica*, an album whose hazy loops of feedback and ululating bass guitar conjured visions of sun-warmed ice. Another Darla title I played repeatedly was Tomorrowland's *Stereoscopic Soundwaves*, an album with titles like "Sea of Serenity" and "A Drop of Golden Sun." My favorite Tomorrowland track, "Dustbot," appeared on *The Sequence of the Negative Space Changes* on the Chicago label Kranky, which also specialized in experimental and psychedelic music. This song features oscillating bleats, an undercurrent of morphing synths and rainlike static, followed by what I can only describe as the sound of cascading lasers. It is a song—like any of the unnamed tracks on NASA's *Symphonies*—that resists categorization, and whose shape is undefined, amoebic. If, say, "A Hard Day's Night" by the Beatles is a solid, then "Dustbot" is a liquid. Or maybe a plasma. Or maybe an ionized plasma. At any rate, you certainly can't hum it. Like the *Symphonies*, it oozes into and out of your ears.

IX.

When I contact Stephen Baker, Tomorrowland's cofounder, I worry that he will be offended by my use of the term *space rock*. That he will think its corny, an insufficient label for his finely honed art. He is less offended by the *space* than he is by the *rock*. "I never really considered *space rock* to fully apply to what we were doing," he said, "as we weren't really working in the *rock* part of the spectrum, but we played shows with and were certainly fans and friends of bands in that scene. We didn't spend a lot of time categorizing our music, but adjectives like *abstract, amorphous,* and *ambient* were commonly used in reviews around that time."

I had to ask: had Tomorrowland listened to NASA's *Symphonies of the Planets*? Stephen confirmed that they had.

"We named a song on our first EP 'Kepler Planet Harmonies' after finding a recording of Kepler's planetary musical notation—an idea that seems like a precursor to NASA's recording project."

Johannes Kepler was a seventeenth-century astronomer who believed that the arrangement of our solar system was a testament to divine order, and that by studying it, one might see into the mind of God. He was the first to discover that the planets in our solar system move, not in the perfect circles that the Pythagoreans assumed, but in elliptical orbits. He also discovered that planets move fastest the closer they are to the sun (aphelion) and slowest when farthest away (perihelion), and that the angles between these farthest and slowest positions have relationships to inversions on a musical scale.

According to James Connor, author of *Kepler's Witch*, Kepler was as important a figure to astronomy as Copernicus, Galileo, or Newton, who had plenty of reasons to seek order. Disease claimed his first wife and son, and three more children during his second marriage. He was excommunicated from the church he loved and longed to serve. And his mother—a peddler of drugs and remedies—was accused of witchcraft after allegedly feeding her neighbor a bowl of poisonous soup, imprisoned, and subjected to *territio verbalis* or "cognition of torture," during which authorities showed her the tools—"hot irons, the rack, the wheel, and so on"—they claimed to use upon her if she refused to confess, a tactic that ultimately failed, as the woman said, "Do with me what you want. Even if you were to pull one vein after another out of my body, I would have nothing to admit."

Meanwhile, Kepler produced *The Harmony of the World*, a book he considered to be his masterpiece and that revealed three significant laws: that planets' orbits were elliptical, not circular; a line from the planet to the sun sweeps out equal areas in equal times; and the square of a planet's period in years and its distance cubed are proportional. For Kepler, the stars exhibited "harmonic consonances," expressed by the Creator in geometrical proportions of the universe. Therefore, one could explain these proportions of planetary orbits in terms of music. And indeed, Kepler presented in this book a notation of songs for each planet.

Today, there's a telescope in space named Kepler. Its mission? According to NASA's website: "The Kepler spacecraft is monitoring the brightness of more than 150,000 stars in the galaxy. Its data are being used to search for planets and also to monitor the natural oscillations of the stars, the field of asteroseismology. The oscillations lead to minuscule changes or pulses in brightness, and are caused by sound trapped inside the stars." It turns out that each star emits its own particular ring, which asteroseismologists can use to determine the size of the star—as well as its age—by its singing. According to NASA, our universe is producing "an orchestra" of sound.

X.

I grew up in a musical family. My mother played piano for our church and accompanied singers and other musicians—like the diminutive German man who played passionate hymns on his violin—during what our church called "special music." My great-aunt was a beloved teacher of music at Southern Missionary College in Collegedale,

Tennessee. My sister and I both took piano lessons for years. My father played the trombone. His brother was a singer and guitarist in a famous Seventh-day Adventist folk group that had—during the 1960s—capitalized on the popularity of the Kingston Trio.

I'd been raised to believe that there were good sounds and bad sounds, and that the body was a temple and everything you put into it—including music—should be carefully monitored. I believed that every consumable thing in the world, every experience that one could say to have *had*, should be subject to close—if not oppressively microscopic—scrutiny, and that most of the world's merchandise—songs, T-shirts, books, movies, magazines, TV shows, and amusements of any kind—that were pleasing to the eye might double as spring-loaded booby traps set by the Devil himself.

Thus the world was full of sounds that had the power to uplift one's soul, as well as those that could allow demonic forces to hijack your brain. This latter idea posed a dilemma for a boy who was not allowed to listen to rock music and had therefore become so desperate to hear Michael Jackson's *Thriller* that he tape-recorded a Pepsi commercial that featured the tight, syncopated beat to "Billie Jean" and then replayed this in his room while wearing a maroon Gamecocks windbreaker that he pretended was the zippered jacket worn by Jackson during "Beat It."

On the one hand, I didn't see the big deal. On the other hand, I'd grown up listening to adults—the people who were supposed to know stuff—talking about how, before he fell from heaven, taking one third of the angels with him, Satan had been in charge of the heavenly choir. His name back then had been Lucifer. As a child, I'd envisioned a monolithic horde of angels—basically sexless and winged masculine beings in white robes, a terraced group rising sky-high—led by another angelic being who, in pictures in Bible story books I read, wore a frown on his face, and whose dissatisfaction with the way angels sang their songs would eventually morph into a disease of his soul. Lucifer had been, in my mind, a mighty conductor who knew about sounds and how they could be harnessed, and the effects they could have on the human body.

Take drums, for instance. Dr. Juanita McElwain, a Seventh-day Adventist music therapist, and the author of *The Lord Is My Song*—a book that details the dangers of secular music—argues that drums were created by primitive tribes in order to summon evil spirits, and that those who listened to music with percussion were in danger of inadvertently inviting demons into their homes. The human brain, she claimed, was the medium through which God, by way of the Holy Spirit, communicated with humans. Conversely, under the right conditions—such as transcendental meditation, faith healing sessions, and rock concerts, the latter of which had the power to induce "hypnotic trances"—consciousness could be altered, and doorways—through which evil spirits could enter—thrown open.

Like many Adventist writers, Dr. McElwain is deeply indebted to and frequently quotes a woman named Ellen G. White, a nineteenth-century prophetess who overcame serious illness after having been struck in the face with a rock at age nine to experience visions where she traveled through space to Heaven and spoke face to face with Jesus

Christ. Though Sister White was devastated on October 22, 1844—the date that the Millerite Movement, of which she had been a member, predicted Christ would descend from the heavens and carry the redeemed to paradise, a day that would hereafter be described as "The Great Disappointment"—she did not give up on God and, with her husband, founded the Seventh-day Adventist denomination. She spent the rest of her life in service to this church, writing books about Christian living and providing advice on all manner of human enterprises, as well as the sorts of things a good Christian ought to avoid, like the wearing of jewelry, the eating of flesh foods, the reading of novels, the playing of cards, and visiting the theater.

Of music, she wrote:

> The Holy Spirit never reveals itself in ... a bedlam of noise. This is an invention of Satan to cover up his ingenious methods for making of none effect the pure, sincere, elevating, ennobling, sanctifying truth for this time.... A bedlam of noise shocks the senses and perverts that which if conducted aright might be a blessing. The powers of satanic agencies blend with the din and noise, to have a carnival, and this is termed the Holy Spirit's working.

What constitutes a "bedlam of noise" is certainly open to interpretation, and though it's not necessarily clear, the role of music becomes important in an Adventist cosmology, especially since it had been Sister White's idea that Lucifer had been the leader of the heavenly choir. And a demon who understands the power of sound can use it in all kinds of ways to confuse the senses and lead us, like the Pied Piper leading the children from Hamelin, into darkness.

XI.

Whenever my mother heard me listening to something she didn't like, she would ask, "Is that something you should be listening to?" I'd usually respond with "I don't know." But sometimes, in her absence, I'd ask myself the same question. My relationship to music wasn't all that complicated; if I liked the song, I listened. But as a teenager, sometimes the things I liked—Jane's Addiction and Ministry and Skinny Puppy and Nine Inch Nails—made me afraid.

I was afraid of Jane's Addiction because of *Nothing's Shocking*, whose cover features naked female twins with their heads on fire. On the back a photograph of the group makes them seem like a band of gypsies. Perry Farrell has big, crazy-wide eyes, dreadlocks, and the hooked nose of a witch. He's wearing lipstick and eye shadow. He's draped in beads. One of the main reasons I was scared was that I loved the music. It was dark and epic and loud and melodious, and Farrell could howl. But when I looked at the picture on the back, I wondered what it meant that I liked music like that. I wondered if they worshipped the devil, if they'd traded their souls for earthly fame. Maybe I was paying homage to Satan by listening to this music. Could one pay homage to an entity without intending to? I doubted it but worried just the same.

XII.

On the day in Astronomy 101 when Dr. S. had been discussing stellar parallax (otherwise known as the geometric strategy used to determine the distance between Earth and other heavenly objects), I wrote down a question in the margin of my notebook: "Did sin affect the entire solar system?"

I can't remember what I was thinking at the time, if I'd wanted to make a connection between the desolate surfaces of neighboring planets and the consumption of fruit from the Tree of the Knowledge of Good and Evil, but I'm sure of one thing: I was dead serious. I wonder now if I'd heard the *Symphonies* at this time in my life, how I would interpreted them. Would I have found them, as I do now, uplifting? And what of Sister White? What would she have said, had she opportunity to hear this dark, atonal celestial concert? Were they evidence of a universe tainted by sin? A manifestation of chaos that, if listened to for an inordinate length of time, might drive one insane? Or were they merely the ambient sounds of nature, and therefore no more harmful than listening to a summer thunderstorm?

XIII.

Actually, the word *ambient* is often used to describe the more abstract branch of space rock. I relied heavily on the word when I first began trying to talk about this kind of music, which I never did in much detail, because describing music that sounded ambient was next to impossible. So somebody would say, "Hey, you like ambient stuff, right?" and I would understand the code: that the person was referring not to "background noise" but to something that sounded like Brian Eno's *Music for Airports*. Something discreet, possibly rhythmic, and unobtrusively so. Something you could forget about, but whose melodic sound-baths lent a beatific atmosphere to the day's activities.

I figured the origin of *ambient* would have something to do with quietude or hypnosis or—like the sleep-inducing drug Ambien—deep and uninterrupted slumber. But the

Latin *ambient* is the past participle of *ambire*, which means "to go." The more I thought about it, the more appropriate this definition seemed. Ambient music serves well as background music, the kind of thing you put on and forget about once it has discreetly drowned out the rest of the world, but it can also be fuel for daydreams, for wanderings and detachments from one's present reality. Try, for instance, to play Flying Saucer Attack's "To the Shore" with your eyes closed and *not* go somewhere: a series of clamorous gong strikes gives way to the rhythmic thwacking of a guitar pick against muted strings, followed by the metallic crash of a ride cymbal and a mournful, loon-like horn. Listening to this song—a cacophonous, if vaguely melodic storm—is, I'd argue, not unlike drifting into benign and rather pleasant insanity.

One can achieve similar effects by listening to the *Symphonies*. On some level, sure, it might be described as "a bedlam of noise." Then again, much of what we encounter in nature has no discernible melody, and yet we find it soothing. Wind. Rain. Ocean waves. And maybe our brains have been hardwired to respond positively to these kinds of sounds. After all, we've been listening since before we were born, when the burbling of our mother's digestive system, the resonance of her voice, and the rhythms of her heartbeat composed our very first symphony.

XIV.

In the *N* section of a Wikipedia page that compiles a list of notable artists who compose, or have composed, "dark ambient music" at some point in their careers, NASA appears second, behind Nadja and Necrophorus. (The

Ns also include Neptune Towers, Nocturnal Emission, Noisegate, and Nurse with Wound.)

NASA is a governmental agency. As such, it is not a person. It is clearly not—if I may be so bold to say—an artist. And neither was Fred Scarf, PhD, the physicist to whose memory the *Symphonies of the Planets* were dedicated, and who, according to the album's liner notes, "developed the acoustic recording project for *Voyager* and is directly responsible for the sounds you hear on these recordings from space." In a 1981 article from *Christian Science Monitor*, Scarf describes the instrument with which he recorded these radio frequencies—otherwise known as the Plasma Wave Detector—as a "sort of car radio antennae hooked up to a tape recorder." The captured data were then processed by Scarf with a microcomputer and synthesizer, resulting in "delicate, crystalline tones; bird-like chirps; deep, booming notes, and piercing whistles weav[ing] ... complex and haunting patterns."

But Dr. Scarf wasn't the first person to attach a recording device to one of NASA's satellites. That distinction belongs to one of his former colleagues, a man named Donald Gurnett, a professor at the University of Iowa. In 1962, Gurnett was an engineering graduate student mentored by James Van Allen, a man who had recently discovered the now-famous Van Allen Radiation Belt, which, according to *Encyclopedia Britannica*, consists of "doughnut-shaped zones of highly energetic charged particles trapped at high altitudes in the magnetic field of Earth," and which helps to protect our planet from harmful solar radiation. Gurnett had been inspired by Roger Gallet, a scientist who'd come to Iowa to deliver a lecture in which he talked about having built receivers that would help him study "whistlers"—frequencies emitted during a lightning flash. Dr. Gurnett defines whistlers on his website:

> Whistlers are produced by lightning. When lightning strikes, electrical energy flows through the glowing gas that we see as a lightning flash. This energy is radiated as electromagnetic waves over a very broad spectrum of frequencies, from very low-frequency radio waves to visual light. The lowest frequencies are well within the audio frequency range. Some of these radio waves propagate upward into the ionized gas (plasma) that exists above Earth's atmosphere. As the waves propagate through the plasma, they are guided along Earth's magnetic field, and often echo back and forth between the northern and southern hemispheres. The waves travel faster at higher frequencies and slower at lower frequencies. Therefore, a spacecraft will first detect the higher frequencies and later the lower frequencies. The result is a whistling tone, hence the name "whistler."

In 1962, Gurnett built a receiver in the basement of the University of Iowa physics department, then took it to his parents' farm in Fairfax. He shut off the electricity in the house, to reduce interference. Then he took his device into a nearby field and waited. He heard only wind and crickets and night sounds. The next night he tried again. He waited for hours. Finally, he heard a dopplering, high-pitched sound. A whistler.

Fifty years later, I talked by phone to Dr. Gurnett, who explained that—other than the sounds made by humans and animals—there aren't all that many "natural" sounds to hear on earth. Wind blowing through trees. Thunder. Waves on the beach. Rain. Falling ice. But that's about it.

In space, however, it turns out that plasma (that is, ionized gas) has various modes of propagation and thus creates a wide array of soundwaves. Dr. Gurnett implored me to visit his website, where he has catalogued these events in a section he calls "Sounds of Space." Here one can listen to the satellite *Cassini*'s recording of lighting on Saturn, *Voyager*'s "termination shock," auroral radio emissions, and Jovian bow shock. And whistlers.

A whistler, as it turns out, sounds a lot like a direct energy weapon—i.e., a phaser—from *Star Trek*. Round up enough whistlers and play them on repeat, and you'll have something that will resemble the "laser cascade" in Tomorrowland's "Dustbot." Actually, take almost any sound effect ever produced in a film or television show that represents space or space travel—the bleeping dashboard on the *Enterprise*, a Tie fighter's terrifying scream, the singsongy tweet of UFOs in any number of 1950s B-movies, the hum and crash and snap of light sabers, or the inexplicable noises made by alien creatures—and you can find their analogues somewhere in space, whether it be a magnetosphere, ionized gas, or radio emissions. Which might mean that the stuff that sounds "spaciest" to us does so for a reason: these are the exact sounds that space itself has always been making and is still making, right now.

XV.

Not long after Gurnett recorded whistlers, he became a project engineer for *Ingun 3*, the first university-designed spacecraft, and asked Van Allen if he could place his recording device on it. Abigail Foerstner, in her book *James*

Van Allen: The First Eight Billion Miles, writes about what happened once the spacecraft went into orbit:

> Whistlers trapped in the earth's magnetic field sang loud and clear without any of the long periods of silence that had frustrated Gurnett's tests with the receiver on the farm. "Instead, we had this tremendous chorus of strange signals and all sorts of radio phenomena that frankly had never been heard before," Gurnett said. British researchers coined the term *dawn chorus* to describe a steady stream of natural radio tones from space because the concert of sounds reminded them of the chorus of chirps sung by birds when they awake at dawn. But no one could account for all of them. Now Gurnett, Van Allen, and the Iowa team quickly realized that the "chorus" of VLF radio sounds they were hearing from space could be traced to the radio emissions from electrons in the Van Allen radiation belts. The sounds dramatically changed in pitch and frequency with even mild solar storms, recording how the intensity of radiation in the belts changed in response to events on the sun. The radiation belts literally sang a song composed in outer space.

XVI.

NASA's *Voyager* satellites—*Voyager 1* and *Voyager 2*—are the most distant manmade objects in space. According to the NASA website, these satellites are currently traveling at their maximum speeds of 35,970 mph, which means that they are moving 111.75 times faster than the speed of sound. The satellites have now reached the Heliosheath, that is, "the outermost layer of the heliosphere where the solar wind is slowed by the pressure of interstellar gas."

Both *Voyager 1* and *2* are carrying, as part of their payload, a plasma wave instrument that Donald Gurnett helped engineer. The radio signals emitted by these satellites—which recorded in 2004 the effects of *Voyager 1* as it crossed a band of turbulence caused by solar wind called "termination shock"—now take sixteen hours to reach Earth. The satellites are also carrying a gold-plated copper disc called *The Golden Record*. According to NASA,

> The contents of the record were selected . . . by a committee chaired by Carl Sagan of Cornell University, et al. Dr. Sagan and his associates assembled 115 images and a variety of natural sounds, such as those made by surf, wind and thunder, birds, whales, and other animals. To this they added musical selections from different cultures and eras, and spoken greetings from Earth-people in fifty-five languages, and printed messages from President Carter and U.N. Secretary-General Waldheim. Each record is encased in a protective aluminum jacket, together with a cartridge and a needle. Instructions, in symbolic language, explain the origin of the spacecraft and indicate how the record is to be played. The 115 images are encoded in analog form. The remainder of the record is in audio, designed to be played at 16-2/3 revolutions per minute. It contains the spoken greetings, beginning with Akkadian, which was spoken in Sumer about six thousand years ago, and ending with Wu, a modern Chinese dialect. Following the section on the sounds of Earth, there is an eclectic 90-minute selection of music, including both Eastern and Western classics and a variety of ethnic music. Once the Voyager spacecrafts leave the solar system (by 1990, both will be beyond the orbit of Pluto), they will find themselves in empty space. It will be forty thousand years before they make a close approach to any other planetary system. As Carl Sagan has noted, "The spacecraft will be encountered and the record played only if there are advanced spacefaring civilizations in interstellar space. But the launching of this bottle into the cosmic ocean says something very hopeful about life on this planet."

Some additional facts about *The Golden Record* bear mentioning: the "greetings from 55 languages" section includes the phrases "Hello friends from farland [sic]" in Thai, and "Hello to the residents of far skies" in Persian, and "Greetings from a computer programmer in the small university town of Ithaka on planet Earth" in Swedish, and "How's everyone? We all very much wish to meet you, if you're free, please come and visit" in Mandarin. The "Sounds of Earth" include audio of mud pots, surf, wind, a train, a dog, and a heartbeat. Musical selections feature instruments such as the gamelan, the didgeridoo, and panpipes, and include the "Brandenburg Concerto No. 2 in F" by J. S. Bach, a pygmy girls' initiation song, "Johnny B. Goode" performed by Chuck Berry, "Dark Was the Night, Cold Was the Ground" by Blind Willie Johnson, a night chant by a Navajo tribe, and a Mexican Mariachi song titled "El Cascabel," which is described quite aptly by Timothy Ferris in the book *Murmurs of Earth* as being as "agile as a school of flying fish." Of course, no single record could comprehensively represent the sounds of Earth, but it's difficult to imagine an album doing a better job than this one. Jam-packed with a variety of sound, it would certainly give another intelligent life form plenty to think about. I couldn't help but wonder: How many more years could be expected to elapse before *Voyager* reached a solar system with a planet that might sustain life forms like our own?

Dr. Gurnett told me to take a guess.

I thought for a moment. "Fifty years?" I said.

He chuckled. "Like most people, you guessed on the low end of the spectrum. A more likely timetable would be, oh, somewhere around thirty thousand years."

Don't bother doing the math because you can't. Or maybe you can, but it doesn't help to comprehend the number. Thirty thousand years is *three hundred* centuries. It's four hundred–plus average human lifetimes. Five times the recorded history of humanity. Ten million, nine-hundred-fifty thousand days. You might as well be trying to comprehend eternity. Which is more or less what another race of intelligent life forms will be called to do, supposing they exist and that this record reaches them. How touched would they be upon finding this record, and how sad once *they* did the math—only to understand that the people who sent this gift were long gone.

XVII.

In performing the research for this essay, I looked up my old astronomy T.A. I typed the name—a one Dr. S.—from my notes into a search engine and arrived at a page for a department of physics and astronomy at a Midwestern university. Dr. S.—now an associate professor—wore the same beard, the same smile I couldn't help interpret then (as now) as a little bit smug. I clicked through to his personal home page. My former T.A. was sitting on the curve of an anthropomorphic crescent moon. Stars could be seen where the shadow of the Earth on the satellite's surface would have blotted them out, and the photo's caption read: "Dr. S discovering the anomalous transparency of the moon."

The page listed his email address, so I decided to write him. I reminded him who I was, acknowledged that he probably didn't remember me, but that his class had impacted my life a great deal. I told him that the story he'd told in his class about the origins of the universe had troubled me at the time and reminded him that I'd visited his office hours and asked if he believed in God and that he said no. I also said that I was working on an essay about the *Symphonies of the Planets* and that my views had evolved to a place in which I could both appreciate the findings of science as well as the varieties of religion. And then I wondered if the God question came up in the courses he taught and what he said, and if he had any colleagues who had been able to successfully integrate science and religion. And then I wished him the best.

I am still waiting to hear from him.

XVIII.

Though I hate to acknowledge it, the *Symphonies* may not be for everyone. I came to this realization one morning in a classroom where my wife and I were teaching a Sunday School class at the Episcopal church we attend. I don't recall today why I agreed to do such a thing, in part because I found it next to impossible to talk, with any authority, about God, especially to children. For years, talking about God made me feel like a fraud. I couldn't get past the word *God,* worried that it automatically conjured up some kind of *Far Side*–like white-bearded patriarch. I say now that I believe God exists beyond language, though I hardly know what that means, in part because I am using language to say it. The divine—as far as I can tell—is knowable only as lived experience: the Gospel of John, read aloud and without commentary, by a dozen volunteers in a church after dark; a plate of food, passed from the hand of one person to another; light filtered through leaves; skin on skin; the song of a breath; a sky full of stars.

The Episcopal church we attend is fairly progressive. Until recently, one of our rectors was gay. The rector who served before him was a woman. We've got a Darwin scholar in our midst; once, he played Adam in an Easter pageant. And the guy who's married to our church organist—and who also happens to be a professor of music—sometimes sports a T-shirt that lists the top ten reasons to be an Episcopalian, the last of which claims that, "Whatever you believe, you are guaranteed to find someone who agrees with you." Despite all this, the binder of materials we were given to teach our Sunday School class seemed at times to be a bit oversimplified, if not downright sentimental, and many of the activities that we did—like "open a newspaper and see where you can find God in the headlines," or "show the rest of the group surprising feats you can do with your body, to show that you are 'fearfully and wonderfully made'"— caused me to cringe. I didn't know if middle-schoolers were rolling their eyes behind our backs, or what they thought about what we were doing, in part because they didn't seem interested in sharing what really went on in their heads.

One Sunday, I decided to bring the *Symphonies* along. I'm not sure why; maybe I hoped that they would create a tranquil space wherein we might reflect on the fact that "the heavens declare the glory of God." I insisted that candles be lit, turned off the buzzing fluorescents. I played number three on the disc. Two kids showed up. I asked them what they thought. They said they thought it was creepy.

The truth is that I understand that the *Symphonies* might be terrifying. It's easy to imagine parts of them being played alongside a tense scene in a horror movie. Other times, the *Symphonies* seem ominously grandiose, as if thousands of lost souls are screaming in unison, the wails of a harrowing choir. A galloping fleet of phantasmagoric horses. Howling wind. Pulsing tones. Mindless murmurings. It is the sound of madness. Of derangement. And maybe that's why I like it: it is a manifestation of incoherence. It is chaos contained.

And while you can listen to the *Symphonies of the Planets* and conclude that, as an aural manifestation of chaos, they supply evidence that the universe is godless, I can't help but hear, in their whistles and drones, an invitation to contemplate the divine. As Joy Williams writes, in *99 Stories of God*, "We can never speak about God rationally as we speak about ordinary things, but that does not mean we should give up thinking about God. We must push our minds to the limits of what we could know, descending ever deeper into the darkness of unknowing."

XIX.

We know that everything we see is made up, essentially, of the same stuff. And whether we believe that God called it into being or the universe itself has the requisite "intelligence" to pull itself up by its bootstraps or that it's going to collapse on itself and start over or that we humans were literally formed by a God whom we resemble in physical shape and that He created us, there's one thing we should all be able to agree on: we're all related, in one sense or another. There's a lot of things I don't like to think about and many more I don't understand, but this fact—and it does seem to be a fact—seems not only profoundly sobering but an occasion for joy.

I don't know if I can explain why the *Symphonies*—as sounds that represent the kinds of activities planets have been engaged in since the beginning of time—have the effect of reminding me about this fact, but they do. And as such, they are a call to worship. An entreaty to slow down. To grow solemn. To zone in, not out. To stare through a window and be grateful for what I see and that I am here, if only for a moment, to see it, because what I am seeing is—essentially—me. As Hans Cousto, a Swiss mathematician and musicologist, says: "Being one means being one with the all. To perceive the vibrations and to reverberate with them means to bring your life—or simply yourself—in tune with the all. When the person . . . is in tune with the cosmos, then the cosmos is resonating in the person. When you become aware of this, consciousness reaches cosmic dimensions."

XX.

You might think that I'd grow tired of the *Symphonies*—that listening to a bunch of what most people would consider white noise might wear me down. But here's the thing: I couldn't stop now, even if I wanted to. Because even after I press stop, the *Symphonies* keep on coming. I hear them in the centrifugal whirring of a neighbor's heat pump. The gurgle and hiss of boiling potatoes. The dopplering automobiles on the street outside my house. The purr of a floor heater. The distant hum of a jumbo jet. The faint whistle somewhere inside a gushing showerhead. The clang of metal and the resultant reverberations when I toss a frozen waffle into my toaster oven. The bleeping keyboards and staticky walls of guitar in whatever space rock band I've dialed up. In other words, I hear the *Symphonies* even when they're *not* playing. And they remind me of something: that I—that we—are all, as matter composed of constantly moving particles, vibrating and, on some level, making sounds. Making music. And by *all*, I truly mean birds, trees, reptiles, mammals, tubers, fruits, stones, and leaves. Beneath the everyday soundscape to which we're attuned, a cacophonous recital unfolds. Even now, whether we like it or not, our bodies are singing. Someday, of course, we will die, and the song will change. Things inside us will still be moving. But in a different direction. A different speed. A different rhythm. And it will play a part in composing a different sort of heavenly choir, a hymn whose notes will never be repeated or heard, a song that will be living and dying, like the songs sung by planets: songs that were sung before any of us humans were ever born and will continue long after we're gone, the sound of which is the closest thing to apprehending eternity, and thus the mind—if such a thing could ever be entered—of God, who, according to some of our earliest records, looked down upon all of creation and said it was good.

OVER THE RIVER AND THROUGH THE WOODS

"No matter what happens on this trip," the woman said, "we are going to be nice to each other." She appeared to be addressing the boy in the back seat—a cowlicked towhead who'd protested a rule stipulating that he read for thirty minutes before he played video games—but the man driving the car knew the decree had been directed at him as much as anyone. He didn't like to admit it, but he had a habit of regressing into less appealing versions of himself during these trips to visit his parents, who lived in the mountains, in an imposing brick edifice on a hill above two streams. There, deep in the woods, the man tended to disengage. To brood. To let slacken the supervisory roles he normally assumed regarding the boy's meals and playtime and baths. Moreover, he became oddly dictatorial, making sudden, if presumptuous, proclamations regarding the family's upcoming activities. They would all hike to the waterfall! They would catch and eat a fish from his father's pond! They would watch old videos of his father tormenting— albeit in a good-natured fashion—the man's now-dead grandmother by threatening to liberate a rattlesnake the father had caught and trapped in a plastic bucket! Such behavior not only failed to meet the woman's approval, it lit the relatively short fuse of her temper. And because she—least of anybody—preferred not to be at the mercy of her anger, she had no choice but to launch preemptive strikes against the inevitable.

The woman asked again if the boy—her son—understood what she meant when she said they were all going to get along.

The boy, who was often said to be the spitting image of his father, scowled at the giant cross of the Draper Baptist Church, whose sign reminded the drivers of Interstate 81 that "If the Devil Is Offering You a TREAT, IT'S A TRICK," and opened up a copy of *The Phantom Tollbooth*.

The woman repeated her question.

The boy—albeit resentfully—answered, "Yes."

*

Three months before, the woman had urinated on a plastic wand and discovered that she was, as she'd suspected, pregnant. This was not, as it turned out, an occasion for joy: the woman's last three pregnancies had ended in miscarriages, and the couple had resigned themselves to "not trying," though they now admitted a degree of carelessness in achieving that goal, favoring—as they had when their first son had been conceived—the fabled rhythm method as a contraceptive technique. The woman had delivered her news to the man from the back deck of their house. The man, who'd been raking mown grass into clumps, inquired about the accuracy of the tests. The woman reminded the man that this had been a question he'd asked at the outset of each and every one of her previous pregnancies and assured him that the tests were exceedingly accurate and that she was indeed pregnant and that now she would be going to the drug store to retrieve some pharmaceuticals that, in her current condition, she required. The man resumed his raking. Minutes before, this had been another task to complete before he could return to the work of grading his students' papers. Now the activity seemed infused with import, as it very well might be the moment in a story he told a future child: *I was raking mown grass in the yard when I heard that you might be coming.* He knew he was jumping the gun, that he should avoid rhapsodic overtures in which he imagined what it would be like for his son, who had recently observed two brothers—his friends—tossing a football in a neighboring yard and wished that he too had a sibling, holding a baby sister or brother. Of course, it wouldn't be easy. They'd have to repurchase all the baby products they'd donated to Goodwill over the years—baby backpacks, baby slings, blankets, jammies, playpens, a crib—and they'd have to go through the whole diaper-changing routine again, and they'd have to baby-proof the house, and their schedules, which had finally become predictable, would become again chaotic, and nighttime feedings would transform them into cognition-depleted zombies. Maybe they'd have to dribble the next baby to sleep, as they had the boy: pat the child's back hard enough so his body bounced against the mattress, an odd yet effective palliative. Then again, maybe this next baby wouldn't be as fussy. Wasn't that the way it was with kids, or how people who had more than one kid seemed to talk about the difference between one and the other? If the first gave you trouble, the second would be smooth sailing? Surely, the man thought, he and his wife as experienced parents would be more relaxed—how could they not be, now that they had careers and a house and two cars?—and they'd enjoy it a little more this time around.

Stupid, the man thought. With a rake tine he flicked a desiccated dog turd onto the grass pile. He yanked a black trash bag from the pocket of his shorts and unfolded it by snapping it hard. The bag, filling with air, ballooned.

*

In the car's rear compartment, the family dog panted. Over the past year, the dog had suffered her share of afflictions: excessive shedding, dry skin, weight gain, and a case of fleas so bad it required the calling of a professional exterminator (a hardy man who sprayed every inch of the house in chemicals he swore were safe). Ten months before, the dog had nearly died. She'd stopped eating, lost weight, refused to run, and eventually sequestered herself in her crate. At the veterinarian's office, she was confined to a small cage. A plastic cone around her head prevented her from biting the IV tube in her paw. The boy, upon encountering the pup in this condition, had burst into tears. After a week in the dog hospital and a thousand dollars in tests, the veterinarians pronounced that she had Addison's disease, which was the exact malady about which the woman had initially inquired, having entered the dog's symptoms into a popular Internet search engine and analyzed the results. The doctors did not apologize. The man and woman thought about delivering a letter of complaint, but—perhaps because they were already burdened by bureaucratic language of recommendation letters and course proposals and dossiers—they procrastinated writing it, long enough that the act lost all its urgent energy. The important thing was that the dog was not going to die, that she would indeed be completely fine—as long as she took steroids every day for the rest of her life. Once, she'd been passive and sulky when other dogs barked at her during walks. Now, her hackles rose like porcupine quills and she lunged where savage little mouths appeared in the spaces between fence posts.

*

The man's parents lived half a day away—just long enough to discourage more than a few visits per year: once during the summer and again now in November, during Thanksgiving Break. To distract himself from the interminable passage of time spent behind the wheel, the man played an audiobook he'd downloaded onto his smartphone, which was now connected to the car's radio through a USB port. This particular book concerned itself with a number of historical events leading up to World War II. Each of the book's sections began with a proper name, like "Winston Churchill" or "Adolf Hitler" or "Joseph Goebbels" or "Eleanor Roosevelt," then described an action by this particular person. At some point in the narrative a date was supplied, often at each section's end. "It was the summer of 1929," the narrator said. "It was the winter of 1934." Presently, in the hail-damaged CRV in which the family rode, it was less than a month from when the Mayans had supposedly predicted the End of Days, an event that the man had imagined many times during his life, as he'd been raised in a denomination whose evangelic literature favored representations of falling buildings, celestial firestorms, and anguished people—the "wicked"—swallowed by gaping fissures in the earth.

The woman confessed that she wasn't crazy about the audiobook and suggested that next time the man include her in the selection process; together they could choose a title they both might enjoy. The man, gripping tightly the shuddering wheel, rolled his eyes, as if her disapproval was an attempt to reveal an essential character flaw. He didn't love the book either, but he'd resolved to keep listening, an act that had now become problematic; the woman's aversion had negated any possible enjoyment he might get out of it, and he became suspicious of the narrator's every utterance.

*

The woman, to be sure, had more preferences than the man. She was often too cold or—especially after she'd showered and dried her hair—too hot. She did not appreciate public affection nor did she welcome compliments regarding her appearance. She disliked scary movies, overly loud music, and riding in fast cars with the windows down. She abhorred mayonnaise, cold cheese of nearly any variety, glasses of milk, and Alfredo sauce. She asked those who were watching her apply makeup to remove themselves from her presence. She could not bear—not even for a mere thirty seconds—the voice of a single conservative radio host. A jazzman who scatted, who so much as unleashed a single scoob-be-de-do-whop, drove her utterly mad. In the woman's presence, one whistled at one's peril. One certainly did not, if one were in control of the television remote, linger upon a channel that documented for any length of time footage of bloodthirsty cats bringing down luckless ungulates.

Despite this catalog of displeasure, the man could not deny—as much as he sometimes appeared to suggest— that the woman was, when it came right down to it, easy to please. She liked back rubs, funny dances, jokes involving the word *chicken,* a clean house, a good dinner, and finding something entertaining to watch in the evenings. The man knew this. The woman was many things. Mysterious was not one of them.

*

The boy said he was hungry. The man said, "No, you're not." The woman told the man that he didn't know if the boy was hungry or not, that this was the kind of unpleasantness into which she wished the family would avoid descending. The man, who knew for a fact that the boy had not ever been truly hungry in all his life, pointed out that the child had eaten only two hours before. This particular observation fell upon deaf ears.

The boy wanted to go to Taco Bell, a place he preferred over McDonald's, an establishment he prided himself on knowing should be boycotted. On the other hand, he fancied himself adventurous for choosing something called a Beefy 5 Layer Burrito. The man asked the woman to look up Taco Bell on her phone. The woman couldn't find her phone. She couldn't understand; she'd just had it in her hand. The man located his own phone and, despite the fact that the woman had asked him not to mess with it while he was driving, swiped its screen until he landed on an application that located nearby restaurants.

In the next town a Taco Bell–shaped building had been boarded up. The boy was displeased, his parents relieved. They all waited in line at a Wendy's, previously famous for salad bars and baked potatoes. In other words, once upon a time, perfectly reasonable fare. This particular restaurant, however, seemed to be at the mercy of incompetence. The woman's fish filet arrived with a slathering of tartar sauce, a condiment she'd explicitly requested be absent. She asked for a new bun, wiped sludge from the fish patty with a napkin.

A boy—a toddler at another table wearing a camouflage hat—stared at the man. He stared back. The mother of this boy presented him with a platter of fries covered in chili and cheese. She wore purple pants whose rear revealed the word PINK.

The man took the dog next door, to the boarded-up restaurant, commanded that she do her business. Ears flattened to the sides of her skull, she complied. The man stomped an empty can from which he'd guzzled an energy drink. There was no garbage bin, so he slipped the flattened disc into a shrub, told himself to act natural. As if anybody cared. As if the trash police might be watching him through a secret cam and at any moment descend.

*

Since the boy had been born, the woman had been pregnant three times. She'd battled morning sickness, forgone her daily cup of coffee, her evening cocktail. She'd injected herself in the stomach twice a day with anticoagulants. She refrained from taking blood-thinning painkillers for the headaches she suffered from caffeine withdrawal. On each of these previous three occasions, she'd been granted—for eight to fourteen weeks—the symptoms of pregnancy, and each time, the fetus inside her had died. Once, on the day before Valentine's, their doctor, who'd been conducting an ultrasound, had informed the man and woman that she could not detect the baby's heartbeat. The doctor said she was sorry, that she would have to perform a dilation and curettage, which would involve, in layman's terms, scraping and vacuuming the dead fetus from the woman's uterus. In the meantime, the woman would have to carry the dead body of what she and the man had hoped might be their next child through that day and the next, during which a winter storm began to sheath trees and power lines in ice. Shards, like bits of broken glass, pelted the windows. They stayed in bed. They waited, held each other, and wept.

*

The man and woman and boy and dog arrived at the man's parents' house in the late afternoon. The house, swallowed by blue shadows, sat on a hill above two creeks, one of which flowed into a pond before meeting with the other to form a larger creek, which wound down the mountain, plunging over boulders and into deep pools.

This house was not the house that the man had grown up in; it was the house his parents had built and moved into after he'd gone away—at fourteen—to boarding school. It was a house whose kitchen drawers and cupboards were filled with candy and cookies and cakes. A house whose antique display cases preserved decorative figurines that appealed especially to those young enough to lack the grace to handle them. A house whose bookshelves offered literature that promoted the byzantine doctrines of the denomination in which the man had been raised. Yet it was, for the most part, cozy. A fire often blazed both in the woodstove and the Rumford fireplace, and the air was often hot and infused, however thinly, with pungent smoke. Though the man's parents refused to get cable, they had a satellite dish for the purposes of receiving transmissions from a television station run by their church. Internet connection lagged. Other than take long walks through the woods or lounge hearthside, there wasn't much to do except sit or talk or raid cookie tins or wait for websites to load.

The house's main room had a vaulted ceiling made of wood. With no separation between the kitchen and this space, which was home to a dining table and an assortment of Barcaloungers, the house became an echo chamber. The phone rang loudly and often: his father's patients calling to report broken crowns, church members delivering information for the man's mother to enter into weekly church bulletins. Upon arrival—or soon thereafter—it was every-man-and-woman-for-his-or-her-self. The man's mother would busy herself in the kitchen. The man's father would bask in the flashing information fields of the Internet. The boy might become bored or rowdy, chasing the dog and nearly crashing into antique display cases housing old dolls and a framed Blue Mountain swallowtail butterfly.

This—passing time idly—was not the manner in which the man and woman were used to being in the world. They had papers to grade, classes to plan, books to read. Emails to compose. Recommendations to submit, on behalf of half-remembered students. Special Topics descriptions—for courses they knew next to nothing about—to construct. Curriculum vitae to update. Grad school applications to rank. Faculty annual reports to maintain. Beyond that, the dog needed to be walked, the laundry folded, the refrigerator restocked. For the boy, there were piano lessons and playdates and soccer practice and Orff music class. The dog's medication needed to be refilled, the cars required new tires, oil changes, inspection stickers. The lawn needed to be mowed or raked or cleared of debris, the gutters cleaned. The lives of the man and woman were ordered, scheduled. The man's parents' home seemed to exist to house long periods of time when nothing special was planned: vast stretches of time where one didn't know what, if anything, to expect.

*

Not long after they'd arrived, the man's mother—a vibrant woman who ate bran muffins during her morning Bible studies and embarked on arduous walks that necessitated the use of featherlight Nordic walking sticks and drank eight glasses of water a day and took vitamins and ate citrus and kale and often popped half an Ambien to ensure eight hours of sleep a night—set upon a search for a casserole she'd prepared for the evening's meal. She could not find it. She opened refrigerators and freezers. She double, then triple-checked. She drove down the road to the empty house where the man's grandmother had lived before she died, to visit the freezer in the garage, which she often used as extra storage. She found nothing. It suddenly occurred to the man that thirty minutes before he had seen—in his peripheral vision—his mother place something into the oven. The man suggested now that she look there. His mother opened the door and—because the casserole was right there, where she'd left it—she began to laugh. The man's mother laughed regularly. He had theorized—until recently, when after experiencing some short-term memory loss, she had been subjected to a battery of patronizing tests and puzzles and math games, leading doctors to conclude that the small black spot in her brain had been the result of a stroke so small it'd gone undetected—that maybe laughing would be the thing to keep her young forever.

*

Both of the woman's parents were dead. When she was fourteen, her mother had died, following a long battle with breast cancer. The woman, then merely a girl, had prayed every night that her mother would live, and nobody in her family had acted as if she wouldn't. The man thinks about this from time to time, and when he does, he remembers a story the woman told him about a woman her father had been dating not long after the woman's mother had died and how this new woman had brought an ice cream pie to the house and how the girl had been so sad and missed her mother so much and that she had sat down in front of the television and eaten that entire pie while tears streamed down her face.

The woman's father had died one year before. He had been carrying a sack of barbecue through a carport and fell and hit his head and began to bleed profusely. He managed to lift himself up again into the living room to sit down. His wife—the woman's stepmother—came home and saw him bloodied and wept. At the hospital, doctors gave a grave proclamation: the man had liver disease. For who knows how long, he had been guzzling fifths of vodka in his truck on his way home from work. One day he was up and about; the next, he lay in a nursing home with his teeth out and a cup of Jell-O fed to him by his wife—a woman whose wardrobe favored animal prints and who seemed comfortable only when filling the world around her with idle chitchat.

The man thought about asking his wife if she was thinking of her father but he didn't. The woman had loved her father though he hadn't always been kind. He was dead now. That part of her life was over. There was, it seemed, nothing more to discuss.

*

In the oven, the casserole began to heat. Meanwhile, the man's father said he wanted to show the man something on the Internet. He often wanted to show the man something: acrobats juggling chainsaws, downhill skiers leaping off rock faces, skateboarding toddlers, snake handlers.

"Look," the man's father said. It was a movie of the man's father's best friend, a bald man with kind, squinty eyes who had once owned a filling station but now was dying of cancer. The man's sister's husband—an artist and graphic designer and filmmaker with a collection of expensive cameras—had recently visited the dying man's living room and filmed him as he talked, in a breathless and wheezing voice, about his life. In the final version of the film, the sister's husband had chosen a few short anecdotes and interspersed these with a variety of images that might be associated with the kind of man who had spent his entire life in the mountains: frosted autumn fields framed by lichen-swabbed fence posts; Sears family portraits hanging on wood-paneled walls; a yellow shopping basket filled with dirt-smudged potatoes; the golden pendulum of a ticking clock; a basket of apples; a bent license plate; a stack of wood beneath a crenellated metal roof dripping with rainwater; a footbridge leading over a creek; a close-up of a photo of the dying man in his younger years, holding the reins of a horse as it towed a giant tree trunk across a field.

The dying man reminisced about getting into a fight with his brother; they'd fought so hard that, according to the dying man, he "couldn't comb his hair for a week." The dying man remembered, with teary eyes, the day that he'd been saved at church. He recalled with fondness a horse that was faster than the wind, a beast who'd never in his life lost a race.

Watching the film made the man sad. He thought of the times that he and his father had visited the dying man's filling station and the shop behind his house. The man remembered a Murphy's Law calendar tacked above a desk—the one where each month featured a chimpanzee dressed in human clothes engaged in some human enterprise: getting married, drinking coffee behind a desk, pushing a shopping cart. He remembered the pink Gojo soap dispenser above a sink. He remembered tools hanging from a wall like medieval weapons. The dying man had once been full of vitality. He could make woodstoves and grade driveways and restore vintage tractors.

The man's father clicked on a button titled "Stats." It displayed a graph that tracked the number of times the movie had been viewed: 4,321 times in the past week alone. The man's father said that the dying man was proud of that. The man supposed that he would be. He wondered how many people would know, after watching, that the dying man was on his last leg. Nothing in the film had suggested he was.

*

Neither the man nor the woman had told a single friend or family member about the pregnancy. And when the boy had seen the bruises on his mother's stomach—the purple splotches that appeared wherever she'd shot herself in the belly with Lovenox, a drug whose name suggested both adoration and treachery—and he'd asked what had happened, she'd told him she'd accidentally run into a door, and he'd put his arms around her and said he was sorry, and the woman told him it was okay, that even though it looked like it hurt, it hadn't.

They'd visited the doctor in secret, dropping the boy off at a neighbor's house, explaining that they had a meeting to attend, which, all things considered, wasn't untrue. At the office the man and woman had sat in a waiting room whose walls displayed artistic renderings of angelic-looking women cradling babies in their arms. They'd walked down a hall where hundreds of anonymous, lizard-faced newborns gazed blindly outward. They'd spied a photograph of the sunburned doctor aboard his yacht, posing with his own four children. A flume of jealousy rose in the man's chest. A young, ponytailed technician—wearing a smock patterned with images of teddy bears—slid a wand into the woman. The man and woman listened to the baby's heartbeat: an oscillating digital pulse. They'd watched a blob on a screen. The man reminded himself of an art installation in the Peabody Essex Museum in Salem, Massachusetts, that had depicted, using hundreds of framed portraits, a small fraction of the government-mandated three-personed families of China. He told himself he'd be fine no matter what happened. As if he had a choice in the matter.

*

The man's mother cut the baked casserole into slabs; the family gathered around the table. The man's father prayed the same prayer he always prayed—more or less—thanking God for the food and requesting that He bless it to the nourishment and strength of their bodies.

The boy took a bite of his casserole. Then he set down his fork and made a face.

"You don't like it?" the man's mother said. "Grandma baked it just for you."

"It has nuts in it," the boy said. The boy was not a poor eater. He ate chicken, steak, hamburger, pork, salmon. He ate broccoli and asparagus. He ate potatoes and rice. He ate bananas and apples and clementines. He even ate peanuts and almonds. But he did not eat casseroles, perhaps because neither the man nor woman ever made them. But the man's mother did. She made a great many things that, while familiar to the man, would be unfamiliar to others. Cooked peaches over toast smeared with peanut butter. Warm lentils poured onto bread, then topped with lettuce and cheese and tomatoes. The man's great-grandmother had written a vegetarian cookbook in the middle of the twentieth century titled *Food for Your Health and Efficiency*. It was nothing if not practical. Before this great-grandmother had died, the man had enjoyed a brief correspondence with her, during which she had inquired about the changing of autumn leaves and if he knew about the necessary effects of chlorophyll.

"Oh!" the man's mother exclaimed. "Nuts are good for you!" she cackled.

"Eat two more bites," the woman said. "And if you're still hungry, your dad will make you something."

"I will?" the man said.

"Yes," the woman said.

"He can eat what he's been given."

The woman shot him a look. The man could tell that she'd already predicted that this would devolve into a fight, and he resented her for having lost faith in him. The truth was, he had already lost faith in himself.

*

The man and woman had agreed: it was time for a vasectomy. The man had made an appointment at a local urologist. In the waiting room he'd admired the Western-style shirt of a scrawny, toothless, big-jawed man whose bouffant might be the result of an extravagant comb-over, and thumbed through the literature handed to him by a blob-shaped woman in maroon scrubs. The brochure's cover featured a middle-aged, middle-class white couple strolling along a beach. Behind them, the crest of a roller coaster rose in the background, as well as a green hill dotted with houses. Above them, the word VASECTOMY hovered—as if to suggest that having oneself neutered was not unlike embarking on a pleasant vacation. Inside the brochure, there was a drawing of a man and a woman relaxing on a bed with coffee mugs and a caption that offered the following advice: "Choosing vasectomy is something you should share with your partner." There were diagrams of an erect penis, testes, prostate, and another diagram of the procedure, during which the vas deferens would be severed. "During surgery," the text of the brochure read, "the two vas deferens are cut and sealed off. This prevents sperm from being able to travel from the testes to the penis. It is the only change in your reproductive system. The testes still produce sperm. But since the sperm have nowhere to go, they die and are absorbed by your body. Only a very small amount of semen is made up of sperm. So after a vasectomy, your semen won't look or feel any different." *Huh*, the man had thought. He was surprised to learn, after all these years, that sperm and semen were two different things. He supposed he had known this at some point. He figured this admission would embarrass his wife, who often inhabited a space of vicarious shame when confronted with the man's refusal to retain basic medical facts. He had envisioned, post-op, a semenless ejaculation, an orgasm without the mess—a member that throbbed to no avail. "Firing blanks" was what he was sure it was called, and therefore that's exactly what he'd imagined: an ejaculation of phantasmagoric proportions. The man flipped the page. Another illustration showed a man reclining in a Barcalounger. He did not appear to be, as the text suggested, icing his balls. He was smiling while his wife offered him a plate of sliced apples. The man wondered if it was right that a wife should be depicted as a servant. Then he acknowledged that it was problematic to assume that because a wife brought her husband a plate of apple slices that it symbolized submission to a patriarch. Couldn't a woman prepare food for a man that she loved, on the day a doctor had taken a laser and soldered shut the valves enabling him to reproduce?

A nurse opened a door and called out the man's first name, which was a name he didn't go by. It took him a second to realize he was the one she was calling. She asked him to step on a scale. The man weighed in at fifteen pounds more than he would've guessed. It was the boots, he thought. And the coat. And the phone and wallet and keys. It had to be. There's no way he could have weighed so much.

*

The man liked to claim that his least favorite holiday was Thanksgiving, that to celebrate it was to perpetuate a farcical notion of pilgrims and natives. Real pilgrims ate plums, acorns, currants, seal, eel, and the wings of eagles. Such a fuss now, cooking an unsatisfactory bird that everyone required but once a year. No one felt good after eating Thanksgiving dinner. To add insult to injury, they would be eating theirs at the man's parents' house, which sat on land bordering national forest, minutes from a valley that three hundred years before had been teeming with a population of Indians that would've doubled the folk that lived there now. But the majority of those natives had been rounded up and marched, barefoot and bayonet-poked, to Oklahoma. Even their ghosts were long gone.

And yet here he was, slathering a turkey with butter. Meanwhile, his mother checked the recipe she was working on and studied a bowl of melted butter on the countertop. Should she have added that to the cranberry crumble? She couldn't remember. The man told her to add it anyway. A little extra butter wouldn't kill anybody.

*

While the bird browned, the man entered the woods with a machete, an instrument with which over the years he had become conversant. The trail, he thought to himself, was not unlike a sentence in need of revision. The blade *tinged!* as it lopped branches. The dog, who was easily spooked, didn't like the looks of this and lingered ten yards behind. With every hack, the dog backtracked, and the man had to keep coaxing it forward.

The man stopped to investigate a dead tree to whose trunk a yellow shield had been nailed. "Wildlife Sanctuary," it said.

The word *sanctuary* made the man think of the heavenly sanctuary, a place that his parents and sister and aunts and uncles and cousins believed Jesus Christ was now working, going through the books, blotting out the sins of those who had asked forgiveness and passing judgment on those who had not.

The man glanced into the woods rising on either side of him, the gray trunks of poplars and maples and oaks rising from a sea of tropical green rhododendron. He imagined camouflaged hunters waiting in the ridges above. Lips bulging with chaw. Guns loaded. Ready to fire. The man had failed to wear orange. In a clearing he inspected a rusted bucket. Across the creek, a pile of charred logs. The man placed his hands above the pile, detected zero heat. Still, in the presence of evidence that other humans had recently occupied this space, he was afraid to go forward. The woods were silent. Leafless limbs rattled in the breeze. Clouds blotched the blue. The sun was up, but hidden behind ridgelines. He imagined camouflaged locals, hidden. If his eyes were sharp, he could pick them out, like ghosts in a Bev Doolittle painting. He imagined them pulling triggers, not because they thought he was a deer but because they were drunk and filled with the glories of meanness. He turned back. The dog ran away. He followed. His heart was an engine pumping him forward.

*

The doctor who would perform the operation was a thick-bodied, hirsute slab of a man. He employed a euphemism when instructing the man to remove his pants. With his gloved hands, he felt the man's testes, directed him to cut his pubic hair—which, the man realized, had gone untended—and to shave his scrotum. *Wait,* the man wanted to say. *I'm supposed to* shave *my scrotum?* He wanted to ask this question but asking it made him feel ashamed. Did other men regularly—or ever—shave their scrotums? He felt stupid for asking.

*

After Thanksgiving dinner, the man's son was bored, so the man took him on a walk to visit the house of his—the man's—dead grandmother, who had lived a quarter-mile down the road, in a house that had been built for her and her husband after his retirement from medicine, a long and storied career that involved service in the U.S. military during World War II as a major and a physician and a conscientious objector, who following the liberation of a concentration camp had saved the lives of who knew how many prisoners. To enter the house, one had to punch a series of buttons—a code—on a keypad. The son wanted—as always—to press the buttons. The code was 1844. The man didn't know if the keypad had come with that particular code or not. If it had, that would've been quite a coincidence. Eighteen-forty-four was the year when William Miller, an itinerant preacher, had predicted that Jesus Christ would return. His followers—a select few of whom would form the denomination in which the man had been raised—had sold or given away all their earthly possessions. They had waited—some, it was probably falsely reported by reporters delighting in the absurdity, wearing ascension robes—on rocks and cliffs and places where they could see the sky, where they imagined a cloud of angels would bloom. But no cloud appeared. No trumpet blast sounded, no mouths opened in the ground, no dead streamed upward. Instead, everyone who looked forward to that day when their bodies would be translated to the celestial kingdom ended up dying an Earthly death. What remained of them now, if anything, was underground.

The man and his son entered the house. They moved like bandits, opening drawers and closets. So much of the man's grandmother's things were still here: Russian teapots and pitchers on shelves, where the woman had hid money and miniature candy bars, despite the fact that everyone who loved her knew the exact locations of her concealments. Now everything seemed drab and dingy and neglected, as if half-resisting being forgotten. Half-heartedly persisting.

In a drawer the man found a stack of paper torn from a palm-sized notebook. On it in his grandmother's handwriting appeared descriptions of a trip to Ivory Coast, where the man's aunt and uncle had lived thirty years before as missionaries. About Treichville, a famous market in a suburb of Abidjan, she had written: *Tiny stalls. Many white-robed Moslems, all kinds of cloth stores and narrow isles. Colorful dressed women in beautiful prints and head pieces. All the women seemed to be pregnant or have a little one on her back.*

It was not clear who the grandmother was writing for. He supposed it was posterity. Him, now, here. His name, of course, was not anywhere to be seen, but he pocketed the paper just the same.

*

The man stood at the edge of the dock, watching his father toss pellets into the pond. Wherever the pellets landed, water churned. Every once in a while, the image of a fish, an enormous trout, pulsed beneath the surface—like a phantom—then disappeared. The man made a comment about the size of the fish. The man's father confirmed that they were excessively big. The man imagined jumping into the pond, fully clothed. He imagined the trout scattering, then engulfing him, swaddling him in a slick fish cloud. He remained on deck.

The man's father liked to use the man as a sounding board, to test out his theories concerning the realities of the current political landscape. On this particular occasion, the father wanted to talk about the man who owned a popular fast food restaurant and who made donations to organizations that did not support gay marriage. "It's like you can't even have opinions anymore," the man's father said, "unless they're the right ones."

The man's father told him that he recently read the Bible from beginning to end. That it wasn't until eight years ago that he'd actually done that. The man perked up. This was a surprising fact about the father he hadn't known. He thought about the father's Bible, the big thick blue one with his name in gold letters on the front, a malleable rectangle stuffed with old church bulletins, a few photographs, bookmarks, pamphlets, and—for whatever reason—a little card with a cartoon baby on it announcing the details of the man's birth.

The father had discovered something. The one thing, the one pattern that he could point to was that God wanted humans to obey him.

The man did not ask the father what particular critical lens he used to interpret the Bible. Did not ask him what he knew about genres of writing or the conventions therein. Did not mention that many stories in the Bible had antecedents in other, older cultures. Did not point out that the Gospels were written decades after Jesus Christ had died. Didn't offer the perspective that perhaps Revelation was written in order to indict the current culture in which St. John of Patmos resided. Didn't ask his father if he thought maybe the "days" in Genesis were symbolic or that the "Tree of Knowledge of Good and Evil" might be a hint that readers were supposed to think of said tree on allegorical terms. Didn't say that calling something a myth was not necessarily a reductive move, since myths couldn't convey truths. Didn't claim that he basically thought that anything made of language could be called a fiction, because words were symbols standing in for things that weren't actually there, and language was a fluid, unstable sign-system and words had no inherent meaning but instead depended on readers, and one couldn't guarantee that any two readers would agree on the meaning of any one particular word, and that meanings depended on culture and context. That wasn't to say that everything was meaningless. Of course not. On the contrary. The meanings were numerous. Possibly infinite. As precious as gold. Which was one reason that the man didn't say anything about the woman having been pregnant. About another baby's heartbeat disappearing forever. He wasn't sure what it meant, how many meanings it might have, how precious they might be. Whatever those meanings were, he thought, he wanted them for himself.

*

"Goodbye," the man told his father. "Goodbye," he told his mother. The woman and the boy and the dog were already in the car, strapped in, ready to leave, the windshield—previously glazed with a thin, white crust—nearly defrosted. The trip's lunch—turkey sandwiches wrapped in foil, apple slices, a half-eaten bag of potato chips, and individually wrapped chunks of milk chocolate—had been nestled into a repurposed gift bag at the woman's feet. The man didn't know it would be the last time he left the house with a loaf of his mother's bread. Didn't know his father would teach himself the recipe once she could no longer navigate its steps. Didn't know that a year from now the simple act of refilling the hummingbird feeder—four cups water, heated, one cup sugar, added—would so badly flummox her that she'd devolve into tears. So he took no special interest in saying goodbye, savored little about having visited. There was only the long drive ahead, which he promised not to dread, previewing instead the joy of arriving at the house where he lived with his wife and son and dog, anticipating the gratitude of opening doors to find things exactly as they had been left, anchoring him to the illusion that this was the place to which they could always return, where things would always be the same.

*

Two weeks before Christmas, the man went in for the operation. He'd taken a Valium in the parking lot. He'd filled a prescription for Loritab. Now he lay in a disposable robe upon a table. Paper rustled beneath him. The doctor appeared. Did the man mind if a medical student observed? The man did not. He hoped he had sheared himself adequately, that the doctor would not order a nurse to come clean him up. The phrase *sheared loins* passed through his mind. The doctors began their procedures. They told him he might feel a prick. Smoke rose from between his legs. The man thought of babies, of the heartbeat they had failed to hear the last time he and his wife went in for an ultrasound, the digital smears their unborn and in fact soon-to-be-dead children made on the black-and-white photos they walked out with. Soon, he thought, it would all be over. The operation would be complete. There would be no more babies. There would be no more dead babies. He would be transformed. He would be a man who could not reproduce. That would be okay. He had reproduced once. Once was enough. Unless, of course, something happened to the one. His wife had said that if something ever happened to their son—that is, if he died—she might have no other choice than to kill herself. He didn't know if he believed that or not. He had heard recently on the radio a mother who had lost a daughter in a school shooting say that she'd thought she would kill herself if anything happened to her daughter and then the shooting happened and the daughter died and the mother decided, in the end, not to kill herself, decided to choose life over death. The man didn't think he would kill himself. At least that's what he liked to think. He would, at the very least, need to get some grieving done. As the doctors worked, a chemical smoke threaded upwards from his groin to the ceiling. He thought about a picture from a storybook he'd read as a child, where the prophet Elijah had placed an offering on an altar, and fire had come down from heaven to ignite it. It was, he thought, difficult to account for what came into one's mind, but he was fine with the image. It was part of the reason he had named his son after the prophet—the one who was minding his own business when suddenly a chariot of fire and horses appeared and swept him up in a whirlwind to heaven. The man had joked that he had wanted to give his son something to live up to. He wondered if his son remembered this story about the prophet who shared his name, the one who never tasted death, and kind of hoped he hadn't. It was a good story, the man thought, and he wanted to tell it again, as if for the first time.

ABOUT THE AUTHOR

Matthew Vollmer is the author of two short-story collections—*Future Missionaries of America* and *Gateway to Paradise*—as well as two previous collections of essays—*inscriptions for headstones* and *Permanent Exhibit*. He was the editor of *A Book of Uncommon Prayer*, which collects invocations from more than sixty acclaimed and emerging authors, and served as coeditor of *Fakes: An Anthology of Pseudo-Interviews, Faux-Lectures, Quasi-Letters, "Found" Texts, and Other Fraudulent Artifacts*. His work has appeared in venues such as *Paris Review, Glimmer Train, Ploughshares, Tin House, Oxford American, The Sun, The Pushcart Prize* anthology, and *Best American Essays*. He teaches at Virginia Tech, where he is Professor of English.

CPSIA information can be obtained
at www.ICGtesting.com
Printed in the USA
LVHW010512150322
713472LV00005B/302